A Slap in the Face

A Slap in the Face

Why Insults Hurt—And Why They Shouldn't

William B. Irvine

OXFORD
UNIVERSITY PRESS

OXFORD

UNIVERSITY PRESS

Oxford University Press is a department of the
University of Oxford. It furthers the University's objective
of excellence in research, scholarship, and education
by publishing worldwide

Oxford   New York

Auckland   Cape Town   Dar es Salaam   Hong Kong   Karachi
Kuala Lumpur   Madrid   Melbourne   Mexico City   Nairobi
New Delhi   Shanghai   Taipei   Toronto

With offices in

Argentina   Austria   Brazil   Chile   Czech Republic   France   Greece
Guatemala   Hungary   Italy   Japan   Poland   Portugal   Singapore
South Korea   Switzerland   Thailand   Turkey   Ukraine   Vietnam

Oxford is a registered trade mark of Oxford University Press
in the UK and certain other countries

Published in the United States of America by
Oxford University Press
198 Madison Avenue, New York, NY 10016

Library of Congress Cataloging-in-Publication Data
Irvine, William Braxton, 1952-
A slap in the face : why insults hurt—and
why they shouldn't / William B. Irvine.
p.   cm.
Includes bibliographical references.
ISBN 978-0-19-993445-4 (alk. paper)—ISBN 978-0-19-993446-1 (updf)
1. Resilience (Personality trait)   2. Invective.   I. Title.
BF698.35.R47I78 2013
155.2'32—dc23   2012021464

1 3 5 7 9 8 6 4 2

Printed in the United States of America
on acid-free paper

CONTENTS

PART THREE
DEALING WITH INSULTS

A Slap in the Face

CHAPTER 1

Introduction

IN THE 1920S, a group of writers, editors, critics, and actors were in the habit of meeting for lunch at the Algonquin Hotel in New York City. They sat at a round table in the hotel's restaurant and, preferably over martinis, swapped witticisms.

Playwright Marc Connelly was a member of the Algonquin Round Table, as the group was known. One day he was sitting at lunch when another man came up behind him, rubbed his hands over Connelly's bald head, and said, "Marc, your head feels as smooth as my wife's ass." Connelly reached up, felt his own scalp, and without missing a beat replied, "So it does, so it does."[1] This is a delightful example of repartee: an insulted person quickly turns the insult back on the insulter. This bit of repartee was sufficiently witty that we are still repeating it eight decades later.

In other cases, the consequences of an insult, rather than being humorous, are horrific. In 1996, for example, Ronald Shanabarger's girlfriend refused to cut short a cruise to come comfort him when his father died. He felt sufficiently insulted by this refusal that he apparently hatched a cold-blooded plan for revenge. He married the girlfriend, had a child by her, and allowed sufficient time for her to bond with the child—all so he could kill the child: he suffocated it with plastic wrap. Doing this, he thought, would make the woman understand how he felt when his father died and thereby make her appreciate the gravity of her failure to comfort him at that time.[2]

Notice that in this case, what Shanabarger took to be insulting wasn't something his girlfriend said and wasn't even something she did; it was something she failed to do—namely, cut her cruise short. Notice, too, that the girlfriend might not have intended to hurt Shanabarger's feelings; to the contrary, she might simply have been thoughtless. We should not make the mistake, then, of thinking that only intentionally hurtful remarks can count as insults. Rather, if you find my behavior to be insulting, I have insulted you, perhaps without intending to do so.

Insults are ubiquitous. It may be uncommon for a boss or teacher to insult us by calling us a fool in public, but insults from friends and relatives are commonplace. They might tell us that the glare from our bald head is ruining the group photo they are trying to take. Or they might tell those present, as we are paying for their dinner, that such generosity on our part is astonishing and suggest that we must be experiencing the early symptoms of food poisoning. Curiously, friends and relatives say these things not because they want to offend us but because they like us and want us to like them in turn. Indeed, if we take offense at what they say, they will be surprised. "We were just teasing you," they will explain.

Another form of insult is simultaneously more subtle and sinister than this. Suppose I tell you that a mutual friend has told me that you are a pompous fool. The friend has clearly insulted you, albeit behind your back. But besides this insult, there might be a second and arguably more malicious insult. Consider, after all, my motives in telling you about the friend's comment. It could be that I did so for your own good: I wanted to let you know that you should not trust this "friend." It is also possible, though, that my motives in reporting the insult are anything but benevolent: I might have wanted to inflict the pain of an insult on you without myself being the author of that insult and therefore without laying myself open to retaliation on your part. Indeed, if I dislike you, hearing someone insult you behind your back is cause for celebration, inasmuch as it presents me with the insult-equivalent of a free lunch.

An examination of insults gives us valuable insight into the human condition. We are people who need to be among people. The problem is that once we are among them, we feel compelled to sort ourselves into social hierarchies. If we were wolves, we might accomplish this with a series of fights: whoever defeated all comers would be the leader of the pack, and whoever was defeated by all would be the last to eat—if any food was left. But we are not wolves; we are instead creatures who have evolved oversized brains, and we have used these brains to develop language. As a result, we don't need to use our teeth or fists to sort ourselves into social hierarchies. We can instead use words, strung together to form insults. And so we do.

TURNING OUR ATTENTION to the historical record, we find that as long as humans have possessed written language, we have used it to insult each other. Thus, in the Old Testament, we find individuals complaining to God about having been insulted: "I am a worm, not a man, abused by all men, scorned by the people. All who see me jeer at me, make mouths at me and wag their heads."[3] We find advice on what to do when insulted: "A clever man slighted conceals his feelings."[4] We find people insulting the Lord: "Remember, O Lord, the taunts of the enemy, the scorn a savage nation pours on thy name."[5] And we find Jeremiah reporting what the Lord told him regarding Israel: "Do you see what apostate Israel did? She went up to every hill-top and under every spreading tree, and there she played the whore."[6] That an omnipotent and perfectly good being would feel the need to insult mere mortals says something about how tempting it is to use words to inflict pain.

Among the ruins of the city of Pompeii, which was destroyed by a volcanic eruption in 79 AD, we gain further insight into the role insults played in the ancient world. Among the graffiti found on the ash-entombed walls of the city, someone carved: "Lucius Istacidius, I regard as a stranger anyone who doesn't invite me to dinner."[7] This comment reveals that in ancient Pompeii, you could insult someone by failing to invite him to dinner. It also tells us that one way ancient Pompeiians responded to insults was to give someone the cold shoulder—to treat him, that is, as a stranger. From a distance of nearly two millennia, this instance of hurt feelings seems ridiculously petty, and yet, we need only look around us to find instances of people in our midst—and possibly even we ourselves—being similarly hurt by similar social oversights.

Notice that in the case just described, the offended person decided to inform Lucius Istacidius of his offense in an anonymous manner. There would have been, after all, a great many people Lucius had failed to invite to dinner; the graffiti leaves him guessing exactly which uninvited individual wrote it. Notice, too, that instead of sending an anonymous letter to Lucius, the offended person posted a graffiti that could be read by everyone. He apparently wanted the world at large to know of Lucius's shortcomings as a host.

At about this same time, in nearby Rome, the Stoic philosophers were analyzing insults and the role they play in relationships. We find Seneca listing the insults directed at him: someone openly laughed at his conversation,[8] someone at a party made a joke at his expense, and someone spoke ill of his writings.[9] Much has changed since Seneca's time, but these would all still count as insults. I will have much more to say about the Stoics later on. As we shall see, they possessed remarkable insight into the psychology of insults, and as a result, they are a source of valuable advice on how best to deal with them.

Moving on to Elizabethan times, we come to what some would call the golden age of invective. In Shakespeare's *King Lear*, for example, Kent calls Oswald "a knave; a rascal; an eater of broken meats; a base, proud, shallow, beggarly, three-suited, hundred-pound, filthy, worsted-stocking knave; a lily-liver'd, action-taking, whoreson, glass-gazing, superserviceable, finical rogue; one-trunk-inheriting slave." And after, one hopes, pausing to catch his breath, Kent goes on to describe Oswald as, among other things, a "beggar, coward, pander, and the son and heir of a mongrel bitch."[10]

Curiously, although many of the words used in them may be obsolete, Elizabethan-style insults are still with us. There are several sites on the Internet that will, at the click of a mouse button, generate Elizabethan-sounding insults by stringing together, in semi-random fashion, words of disapproval that were common in Elizabethan times. One such site[11] obligingly labeled me a "gorbellied elf-skinned lewdster!" And if this insult did not sufficiently offend me, it claimed to have 388,943 other insults available that might do the job.

MODERN INSULTS generally aren't as colorful or verbally adroit as Elizabethan insults were, but they nevertheless manage to carry a sting.

Writers tend to be clever people with fragile egos and are therefore a good source of insults. Thus, we find Truman Capote's acerbic assessment of the works of Jack Kerouac: "That's not writing, that's typing."[12] We find Elizabeth Bowen characterizing Aldous Huxley as "the stupid person's idea of a clever person."[13] We find James Dickey declaring that "if it were thought that anything I wrote was influenced by Robert Frost, I would take that particular piece of mine, shred it and flush it down the toilet, hoping not to clog the pipes."[14]

Politicians are another good source of insults. It isn't that they, like writers, have fragile egos; if they did, they couldn't withstand the stress of campaigning. Rather, they insult political opponents because they realize, as H. L. Mencken put it, that "one horse-laugh is worth ten thousand syllogisms."[15] During an election year, voters are consequently treated to an avalanche of slung mud.

We find Abraham Lincoln suggesting that an argument propounded by Stephen A. Douglas "is as thin as the homeopathic soup that was made by boiling the shadow of a pigeon that had been starved to death."[16] We find William Cowper Brann invoking his dog to insult William E. McKinley: "Why, if a man were to call my dog McKinley, and the brute failed to resent to the death the damning insult, I'd drown it."[17] We find Jim Hightower characterizing Dan Quayle as being "so dumb he thinks Cheerios are doughnut seeds,"[18] and Barry Goldwater asserting, of politician William Scott, that "if he were any dumber, he'd be a tree."[19] And, across the Atlantic, we find Winston Churchill characterizing Clement Attlee as "a sheep in sheep's clothing" and as "a modest little man with much to be modest about."[20]

If insults can be amusing, so can people's responses to them. Indeed, many insult connoisseurs—myself included—would argue that the highest form of insult is repartee. We have already encountered one example of a quick, witty, and insulting reply to an insult: Marc Connelly's quip about his insulter's wife's derrière. For another example, consider actress Ilka Chase's response to Humphrey Bogart when, after telling her how much he had enjoyed her most recent book, he asked, "By the way, who wrote it for you?" Chase, annoyed by the suggestion that she had employed a ghostwriter, had the presence of mind to offer the following rejoinder: "I'm so glad you liked it. By the way, who read it to you?"[21]

I BECAME INTERESTED in insults while doing research on the Stoic philosophers.[22] They spent a considerable amount of time, as I have said, thinking about insults and how best to deal with them. I thought this was an odd thing for philosophers to do but ultimately concluded that they were on to something. If one role of philosophers is to teach us how to have a good life, then it is entirely appropriate for them to ponder insults and the role they play in human affairs. After all, insults have the power to make us miserable.

As a result of reading the Stoics, I became a collector of insults. I started paying attention to the insulting things other people say and do. Blatant, vicious insults, I discovered, are rare; blatant but benign insults, though, turn out to be commonplace: people use them, as I have said, to tease friends and relatives. I also found that insults can be easy to misconstrue: what sounds like praise, for example, might in fact be a cleverly packaged insult.

In the course of my investigation of insults, I made a disturbing discovery: I myself was the source of many insults. For one thing, I became fully aware of how many blatant, albeit benign, insults I unleash in the course of a day. It is not unusual, for example, for me to tease friends. Thus, I might playfully refer to a taciturn friend as a chatterbox, and he might respond, again playfully, by referring to me as "the absentminded professor." But besides these playful insults, I discovered that I am the source of other, more sinister ones. I would analyze conversations I had, only to realize that some of the things I had said could best be understood as subtle attempts to put other people down.

In one such case, a student told me of his plan to pursue graduate studies and asked what I thought of the university he would attend. I replied that the university in question was a real bargain, as graduate schools go. It was only later, when I replayed the conversation in my mind, that I realized that I had, albeit obliquely, belittled his choice of schools. For one thing, my response implied that the school he would attend is where you go if you lack the money for a proper education. My response, in other words, expressed a degree of educational snobbery.

It was clear to me, in afterthought, how I should have responded to this person's announcement—and how I would have responded if I were a better person than I am. I should have congratulated him on achieving what for him was a significant life goal. Not only that, but the congratulations in question should have been heartfelt. And what prevented me from offering sincere congratulations? I must have felt that my own status as an intellectual was somehow threatened by his going to graduate school. "How utterly foolish!" I thought, and felt more than a bit ashamed of myself.

I may be the only person on the planet to engage in this sort of ego defense and petty social jockeying, but I don't think so. We all want other people to know and appreciate how wonderful we are, and one way to accomplish this is by making them realize how relatively insignificant they are. And so we go out of our way, often subconsciously, to inflict subtle insults that will put them in their place.

IT IS OBVIOUS that we insult someone when we intentionally cause him pain by something we say or do. But we also insult him when we cause him pain by something we *refuse to* say or do (such as refusing to shake his hand), or even by something we *fail to* say or do (such as forgetting to thank him for a gift). Indeed, as we shall see, it is not only possible but surprisingly easy to insult other people in the act of attempting to praise them.

If our goal, then, is to go through life causing the least pain possible to those around us, it is important that we gain a deep understanding of insults. More generally, if we wish to understand the human condition, we would do well to investigate insults and the role they play in human relations. In our investigation, we will want to answer a number of questions. Why do we insult each other? Why are insults capable of causing us such pain? Is there anything we can do to prevent or lessen this pain? And perhaps most important, how can we overcome our propensity to insult others? It was with these questions in mind that I wrote this book.

Let me make it clear at the outset that this is not an "insult book" in the ordinary sense of the phrase. Rather than being a book *of* insults, it is a book *about* insults—about the psychology behind them and the social role they play.

In part one of this book I describe the insult arsenal, beginning, in chapter 2, with blatant insults, such as when someone walks up to you and calls you a fat, lazy toad. In chapters 3 and 4, I consider more subtle forms of invective, such as when someone insults you by failing to remember your name or by praising you in a manner in which you don't want to be praised. And in chapter 5, I consider benign insults, such as those involved in playful teasing. These are unleashed not because the insulter wants to hurt his targets, but because he wants to maintain a social relationship with them.

In part two of this book, I investigate the science of insults. More precisely, I turn to psychological research in an attempt to answer three important questions: how much do insults hurt us, who are they most likely to hurt, and why do they hurt? To answer this last question, I turn to the research of evolutionary psychologists. These scientists, as we shall see, maintain that we insult each other in large part because of our evolutionary past: our ancestors who insulted others and were hurt by the insults of others were more likely to survive and reproduce than those who did not, and we modern humans have inherited their psychological propensities.

After this scientific interlude, I turn my attention, in part three, to the advice that has been offered on how best to respond to insults. After describing the various possible responses, I defend the Stoic assertion that the best way to respond to an insult is with no response at all and that if we feel we simply *must* say something in response to an insult, we should respond with words of insult directed not at our insulter but at ourselves—we should respond, that is, with self-deprecating humor. I go on to consider Stoic advice on how to remove the sting from an insult and thereby prevent it from upsetting us. I also investigate the ways in which society has tried to discourage insults—by, for example, adopting codes of politeness and outlawing hate speech.

The goal of this book, then, is not to teach people how to insult others, although as the result of reading it, someone may indeed become more skilled in the art of invective. Nor is it the goal of this book to teach "insult self-defense"—to teach readers, in other words, how to quickly and effectively respond to an insult with a counterinsult. Rather, the goal is to help readers understand insults, the social role they play, the reason we are inclined to insult others, and the reason it hurts when they insult us.

On gaining this understanding, readers might notice, as I have, a change in how they respond to insults. An insult that once would have ruined their day will have lost its sting, and rather than triggering feelings of anger, an insult will trigger feelings of pity toward the person who insulted them. Readers might, as a result, discover that their "insult reflex"—their habit of responding to an insult by insulting their insulter—has atrophied. Likewise, they might notice that they are unleashing fewer "first-strike" insults (against people who have done them no harm) than they formerly did.

It is also possible that as a result of pondering the social function of insults, readers will experience a significant personal transformation. Many readers will have picked up this book because they seek a "cure" for insults; they seek, that is, a prescription that will alleviate the pain caused by the insults directed at them. By the time they finish this book, though, readers might realize that the pain caused by insults is really just a symptom of a far more serious ailment, much as a nagging cough, although itself distressing, can be a symptom of a potentially fatal disease. Readers might also come to realize that in order to increase their chance of having a good life, they should, rather than simply seeking a remedy for the pain of insults, take steps to cure the underlying ailment that causes insults to be painful.

The Stoic philosophers, as we shall see, thought they understood this underlying ailment. They maintained that we insult and are in turn hurt by insults in large part because we have chosen the wrong values by which to live. From this it follows that we can eliminate the pain of insults—and even more important, increase our chance of having a good life—by choosing the proper values. In chapter 11 of this book, I will examine in greater detail the Stoics' "cure" for insults, and in the chapter after that, I will describe the insights I have gained in my own efforts to effect this cure.

Here, in a nutshell, is the predicament in which we humans find ourselves. We are "wired" by our evolutionary past to find some things pleasant, and find other things unpleasant or even painful. In particular, we are wired so that we find it unpleasant to live in social isolation, and so we seek the company of other people. Once among them, we find it unpleasant when they look down on us, socially speaking, and quite pleasant when they look up to us, and so we set out trying to raise ourselves on the social ladder. One of our primary ladder-climbing tools is the insult.

The problem is that the people with whom we deal have this same wiring and as a result, we enter into a social contest with them. The Stoics did not know about the evolutionary wiring I have described, but they understood full well our need to be with other people and the social strife that would ensue when we joined them. It was with this in mind that they developed strategies that would let us enjoy the benefits of human interaction while avoiding much of the pain such interaction could cause. In the pages that follow, I will attempt to reconcile the ancient wisdom of the Stoics with modern scientific research into human behavior.

PART ONE

The Insult Arsenal

CHAPTER 2

Words Like Daggers

As anyone who has been hurt by an insult can tell you, words can be used as weapons. Let us, then, begin our exploration of the insult arsenal. By the time we are finished, readers will appreciate not only the many roles insults play in human interactions but the considerable ingenuity that has been invested in their creation.

Let me preface this exploration with some caveats. To begin with, realize that in the discussions that follow, I am using *insult* in a very broad sense. The dictionary defines an *insult* as "an offensive action or remark."[1] Thus, insults need not be verbal; they can instead involve actions. They can, for example, involve gestures, such as showing someone your middle finger, or they can involve physical contact. This contact might be direct, as when you slap someone, or it might be indirect: if you spit in someone's face, it will be your spit, not you, that comes into contact with him. Furthermore, when a physical insult involves indirect contact, the contact in question can be quite unsubstantial: suppose, for example, you blow cigarette smoke in someone's face or belch in such close proximity to her that she can tell what you had for lunch. In these cases, your insult is transmitted by mere molecules.

The insults just described require us to do something, such as call someone an idiot or blow smoke in her face. It is important to realize, though, that the "action" that constitutes an insult can be a failure to act. Indeed, it is not only possible but surprisingly easy to insult someone not by anything you do but by what you fail to do. Thus, if someone wants or expects to be invited to a party you are giving and you fail to invite her, she will likely feel insulted.

The dictionary goes on to define *offensive* actions and remarks as those that cause anger, resentment, displeasure, or affront. This means that it is possible for something we said or did to count as an insult even though it was not our intent to insult someone. In particular, even though a man didn't intend to forget his wedding anniversary and even though his wife realizes as much, she might nevertheless experience displeasure at the oversight, in which case his behavior will count as insulting. It is also possible for us to insult someone by saying something undeniably true: suppose, for example, I walk up to a bald friend and tell him, truthfully, that "a turkey vulture has more hair than you do." If the remark causes my friend displeasure, it will count, according to the above definition, as an insult. Indeed, even if it is unreasonable for a person to be displeased by what we say, we will, if we displease him, have insulted him.

IT IS IMPORTANT to keep in mind that insults are relative. Thus, words or actions that count as an insult in one culture might not count as an insult in another. In America, for example, you will insult no one—well, almost no one—if you fail to take your shoes off when you enter her house. Do this in Thailand, though, and you will grievously insult your host.

Likewise, words or actions that count as an insult in one subculture within, say, America, might not count as an insult in another. If, for example, you like the motorcycle someone has built or the tattoo he has acquired, you might please him by calling it "sick" or "bad." If, however, an art teacher at a retirement home likes a student's watercolors, it would be unwise for her to refer to them as "sick" or "bad," since the meaning of these colloquialisms would be lost on retirees, and they would therefore take offense. And even within a subculture, whether or not something counts as an insult depends on how sensitive an individual is: a hypersensitive person will be insulted by almost everything we say, but a thick-skinned person will be very difficult to insult.

Furthermore, whether or not something counts as an insult depends on the circumstances. The statement "you are talented and pretty enough to be Miss Montana," said to someone who has just won a beauty pageant in some tiny Montana town, will count as praise. Say the same thing to someone who has just won the Miss America beauty pageant, though, and your remark will probably be construed as an insult. Likewise, if a stranger sits down next to me on the bus and I don't speak to him, it won't—unless he is hypersensitive—count as an insult, but if a neighbor sits down next to me on the bus and I don't speak to him, it almost certainly will count as an insult.

Although what counts as an insult differs from culture to culture, the concept of insulting behavior is universal. It is rare to encounter a human being whose feelings cannot be hurt with a few well-chosen words. It is also rare to encounter a human being who has overcome the temptation, when the opportunity arises, to subject those around him to insults.

Before we humans acquired language, we presumably insulted each other with gestures, body language, or physical contact, the way monkeys do in their attempts to gain social dominance within their troop. The acquisition of language, though, made it much easier for us to insult one another. And with the invention of writing, we gained the ability to insult people at a distance by sending them an insulting letter—or, these days, by creating a website full of insulting comments about them. The discovery of verbal insults tipped the odds, socially speaking, in favor of those who lack physical strength but possess a quick wit: instead of using their fists to socially intimidate others, they could use words that are, as one psychologist has noted, "as easy to deliver as the flick of a tongue."[2] They can also be as cutting as daggers.

THE MOST BASIC KIND of insult is the person-to-person insult. You might first have experienced this sort of insult when you were a child and a sibling called you a dummy or a crybaby. As you grew older, you discovered all the different ways it was possible for one person to insult another. A person insulting you might have attacked you by commenting on your appearance ("you are fat"), your motives ("you are mean"), or your character ("you are lazy"). As you reached adolescence, your enemies might have attacked you by commenting on your past ("you were a bed-wetter") or your sexual identity ("you throw like a girl," said to a boy).

Athletic competitions are often rife with person-to-person insults, as players "talk trash" to their opponents. Their goal in doing this is not to scar these opponents emotionally; rather, it is to "get inside their head"—to fluster them and thereby cause them to play poorly. There was a time when talking trash was considered poor sportsmanship. Muhammad Ali—or Cassius Clay, as he was then known—changed all this. Before, during, and after a fight, he would make belittling remarks about his opponents. Before long, other professional athletes started imitating Ali, and not long after that, amateur athletes followed suit. This trend has continued over recent decades and as a result, we have reached a stage at which the good sportsmanship that used to be ubiquitous on fields of play is on the verge of extinction.

Those wishing to insult someone might engage in name-calling. They might, for example, alter the spelling of his name: if Bob puts on some weight, his buddies might start calling him "Blob." Or they might give him a nickname by adding adjectives to his name: he might become "Big Bob." Or they might abandon Bob's real name altogether in favor of a new name they think is more fitting: if Bob tries to boss his buddies around they might start calling him "Little Hitler," if he lacks the mental wherewithal to graduate from high school they might start calling him "Einstein," and if he refuses to do the foolish things they want to do they might start calling him "Sally."

Parents and teachers are fond of telling children that although sticks and stones can break your bones, names can never hurt you. One suspects, though, that the adults in question would find it more than a little upsetting if one of the children with whom they shared this adage responded by saying, "sure thing, Bozo!" A more useful piece of advice for parents and teachers to be passing along, then, would be something like this: "Sticks and stones can break your bones, but you should develop a strategy to minimize the pain you experience when people call you names." This advice, I might add, anticipates the advice I will be giving later in this book.

Besides insulting Bob by literally calling him a name (such as Sally), Bob's friends can insult him in a metaphorical manner: they can call him something he clearly isn't. They might, for example, call him a chicken, an ass, a dog, a baby, a walking donut, or a whore. Indeed, they can insult him by labeling him to be the exact opposite of what everyone knows he is: if, for example, Bob is a proud teetotaler, they might call him a lush. And if Bob's friends are good at mimicry, they can insult him by mocking the way he walks, talks, or swings a golf club.

Along similar lines, they can, if they are science-minded, "honor" him by naming a unit after him. They might, for example, adopt the "Bob" as a unit of ignorance, which would let them say that a mistake someone made was "two Bobs dumb." A quick check of the Internet, by the way, shows that naming units of ignorance after someone is a popular pastime. Someone has, for example, suggested that we adopt the "Stallone"—after actor Sylvester Stallone—as the unit of ignorance.[3] Elsewhere, a mathematician has dishonored a coworker named Moore by suggesting adoption of the "mooron" as the unit of stupidity.[4]

The insults described above require a degree of wit and effort. It is possible, though, for even a witless, lazy person to insult someone: he need only add a disparaging term such as "dummy" to the things he says to her. Thus, instead of simply telling his sister that it is time for dinner, a child might say, "It's time for dinner, dummy."

One might think that intelligent, articulate individuals would feel no need to insult other people, but they do. They disguise this need by carefully couching the language they use in their insults. Suppose, for example, that after they present a paper on the works of Nietzsche at an academic conference, someone in the audience asks a question that reveals what looks like a critical flaw in the presenter's argument. In this case, the presenter is unlikely to call the questioner a big dummy. He might instead reply by saying, "it is clear that the questioner has not read the works of Nietzsche carefully." The academics in the audience will immediately recognize that the speaker has just called the questioner a big dummy but has done so with style and elegance.

BESIDES VERBAL AND PHYSICAL INSULTS, there are what might be called *quasi-verbal insults*. These insults are not verbal, in the strict etymological sense, inasmuch as they do not employ words. They do, however, involve the production of noises. A person might, for example, make a farting sound (with his mouth) or sigh audibly while someone else is trying to talk. He might laugh or snort in reaction to something someone has said. If he is at a public performance, he might insult the performer by whistling, booing, or hissing.

It is also possible to insult someone with a gesture. Such an insult is not verbal or even quasi-verbal, since it involves no production of noise. Nor is it physical, since it involves no contact—not even with something as unsubstantial as cigarette smoke or the fumes of a belch. Among the arsenal of insulting gestures we find "the bird" (also known as "flipping someone off" or "giving him the finger"), making faces (sticking your tongue out at someone, for example), rolling your eyes, and smirking. And besides insulting someone with gestures, we can insult him by other things we do with our body. We can, for example, pretend to fall asleep while he is talking, we can step on his shadow, and if he is a stranger, we can stare at him and refuse to look away when he makes eye contact with us.

Within the arsenal of insults, we find curious subcategories. Consider, for example, curses. One curse, said to be popular among Gypsies, goes like this: "May you wander over the face of the earth forever, never sleep twice in the same bed, never drink water twice from the same well, and never cross the same river twice in a year."[5] To say this to someone is tantamount to saying that you hate him so much that you hope his life will be miserable. In a lighter vein, consider the following curse, attributed to American naturalist John Burroughs: "May you be cursed with a chronic anxiety about the weather."[6]

Another subcategory of insults involves practical jokes. It is one thing to insult someone by telling her that she has a certain character flaw; it is quite another to demonstrate the existence of that flaw by means of a practical joke. Suppose, then, that Mary's coworkers are convinced that she is a tightwad. As a practical joke, they might glue a dime to the floor. Suppose that when Mary sees the dime, she stoops to pick it up. Suppose, even worse, that she breaks a fingernail trying, unsuccessfully, to get it off the floor. At this point, the coworkers, who had been watching with anticipation, might burst into laughter: "See! We knew it!" When Mary figures out what has happened, she is likely to feel humiliated.

The practical joke just described is hypothetical, but after I mentioned it to a group of students in a presentation about insults and the role they play in human affairs, one student confessed that he had been a coconspirator in a similar practical joke. Instead of involving dimes glued to the floor, it involved a dollar bill smeared with dog feces that had been left for the victim to see. This revelation triggered yet other revelations by the students in the group, and I was treated to a story about a student who surreptitiously put a sign on an overweight student's back, saying "Follow me to Krispy Kreme" and about a student who wrote "Ask if I want beer" on the forehead of a roommate who was sleeping off a drinking binge.

The above practical jokes are crude, to be sure. Other practical jokes are rather more sophisticated. Consider, for example, the pranks the students of Cal Tech and MIT play on each other. In one such prank, students from Cal Tech printed up fake copies of the MIT student newspaper and distributed them around the MIT campus during the weekend that incoming students were making a preview visit. On its front page were emblazoned the headlines, "MIT Invents the Interweb" and "Architects Deem Campus 'Unfortunate.'"[7] The point of such practical jokes is not to achieve social dominance over the students of another campus; it is instead to demonstrate intellectual superiority over them: "How foolish they must be for us to have been able to pull off this prank!"

Practical jokes have a drawback, though: they typically require planning and effort. By way of contrast, verbal insults are best when they are spontaneous and therefore require no planning and little effort. And when a verbal insult is both spontaneous and clever, it will earn the insulter a reputation as a quick wit, something a laboriously planned-out practical joke can't do. It is for this reason that some people look down on practical jokes, even those that are quite clever, as being a lesser form of insult. These same individuals would look down even more on those whose idea of an insult is to swear at someone. Such insults, after all, require zero intelligence.

IN MOST INSULTS we do something to someone. In some insults, though, we don't do anything *to* anyone; we instead refuse to do something *with* someone. Suppose, for example, that when someone offers us his hand, we do nothing in response, making it impossible for him to shake hands with us. He will likely feel highly offended. Other examples of *insults by refusal* include refusing to meet with someone, ride in the same car with him, be in the same room with him, break bread with him, return his greetings, or speak to him. In an extreme case, we might respond to the approach of someone by turning our back on him—by giving him, as they say, the cold shoulder.

Normally, if someone refuses to speak to us, we will take steps to avoid her. Sometimes, though, circumstances make avoidance difficult. Suppose, for example, that we do something to annoy a relative under whose roof we are living and she responds by giving us what is known as the silent treatment: although we live together and eat at the same table, she refuses to speak to us. If communication with us is necessary, it is done through an intermediary: she will ask someone to tell us something. (Thus, the silent treatment and the cold shoulder both involve ignoring someone, but whereas giving someone the cold shoulder means ignoring her in one particular encounter, giving her the silent treatment involves an ongoing refusal to speak to her.) The silent treatment would appear to be a popular social weapon: in one survey of Americans, 67 percent admitted to using it on a loved one, and 75 percent said a loved one had used it on them.[8]

If we live in a close-knit community, the silent treatment might extend beyond relatives: we might find that we are subject to shunning. In Amish communities, for example, people will refuse to have anything to do with a shunned member. It is when others refuse to maintain social relationships with us that we come to realize how much these relationships—that we likely took for granted—mean to us.

The silent treatment and shunning are particularly distressing to those who are subjected to them; indeed, they might experience anger, frustration, and despair so profound that they come to feel that their life has been ruined and along with it, their chances for happiness. And not only is the emotional damage severe, but it can last for decades.[9] It is remarkable that we can inflict this much pain by doing nothing at all.

IN THE PERSON-TO-PERSON INSULTS described above, the target of the insult is some other person. It is also possible, though, for a person-to-person insult to be directed against oneself. And why would anyone want to insult himself? Because it is a singularly effective way to prevent others from insulting him or to deal with the insults they direct at him.

Such self-insults are more commonly described as self-deprecating humor. Along these lines, we find playwright David Niven describing his face as "a cross between two pounds of halibut and an explosion in an old clothes cupboard,"[10] and we find actor Charles Laughton informing us that his face "looks like an elephant's behind."[11] When comedian Joey Adams joked that Ronald Reagan was too old to run for president and cited as supporting evidence that his Social Security number is two, Reagan called to complain: the joke, he said, would be better if the punchline was that his Social Security number is in Roman numerals.[12] Consider, finally, author Graham Greene's response to a contest run by *New Statesman* magazine to come up with the best parody of his writing style. Many authors would resent being mocked in this manner, but Greene responded by entering the contest under a pseudonym. He placed third.[13]

I will have much more to say about self-deprecating humor in chapter 9. As we shall see, if you can make fun of yourself, you make it very difficult for others to make fun of you. In particular, if you describe your face as resembling an elephant's behind, what is left for others to say? By responding to an insult with self-deprecation, you take the wind right out of the sails of those who insult you.

INSTEAD OF HAVING A SINGLE INDIVIDUAL as its target, an insult can be aimed at groups of people. A racist, for example, might aim an insult at not any particular black but all blacks, and a sexist might aim an insult not at one particular woman but all women. Alternatively, among the groups we might insult are those who favor a certain leisure activity (consider, for example, Samuel Johnson's definition of fishing as "a stick and a string, with a worm at one end and a fool at the other."),[14] those who support a certain athletic team (think of the animosity between Yankees fans and Red Sox fans), and those who favor a certain kind of pet (think of the comments dog owners make about cat lovers). If we are college students, we might insult the student bodies of rival colleges ("Harvard students are stuck-up"), the members of rival fraternities ("those Alpha Betas can't hold their liquor"), or those who chose a major other than the one we chose ("math majors are hopeless nerds"). And if we are college professors, we might insult the faculties of other disciplines. Thus, philosophy professors might ridicule marketing professors as a group, who would return the insult, if they had the mental wherewithal to do so.

A group insult can also be geographical in nature. We can, for example, insult the inhabitants of a particular city: Hunter S. Thompson characterized Chicago as being "this vicious, stinking zoo, this mean-grinning, Mace-smelling boneyard of a city: an elegant rockpile of a monument to everything cruel and stupid and corrupt in the human spirit."[15] We can insult the residents of a state: according to Truman Capote, "in California, you lose a point off your I.Q. every year."[16] Or we can insult the citizens of a nation: Napoleon Bonaparte famously characterized England as "a nation of shopkeepers."[17]

When nations are at war, they are particularly inclined to insult the nations they are fighting. During World War II, for example, the warring nations engaged in propaganda campaigns that depicted the populations of enemy nations as being inherently stupid and depraved. Thus, the Japanese soldiers shown on American war posters typically had buck teeth, thick-lensed glasses, and a sinister look. They might also be shown committing some atrocity.

In the same way that individuals can insult themselves, citizens can insult their own nation and nationality. It was, for example, American journalist H. L. Mencken who asserted that "no one ever went broke underestimating the taste of the American public."[18] And it was British novelist D. H. Lawrence who cursed "the blasted, jelly-boned swines, the slimy, the belly-wriggling invertebrates, the miserable sodding rotters, the flaming sods, the sniveling, dribbling, palsied, pulseless lot that make up England." And in case this wasn't insulting enough, he went on to deride, among other things, the quality of Englishmen's sperm.[19]

Other group insults are directed at those who practice a certain profession. Lawyers, as we all know, are much maligned, and although people might be reluctant to insult a lawyer to his face, they delight in coming up with jokes that insult lawyers as a group—jokes like this one: "Why do lawyers make better subjects than rats in laboratory experiments? Because lab assistants are less likely to become attached to lawyers than they are to rats, lawyers breed faster than rats and are in much greater supply, animal rights groups won't criticize you for performing vivisection on a lawyer, and lawyers are more accommodating as research subjects, since there are some things rats just won't do."

While nearly everyone seems to despise the legal profession, some professions are despised primarily by members of other, related professions. Thus, we find movie mogul Jack Warner deriding screenwriters tapping away at their typewriters as "shmucks with Underwoods."[20] We find author Gene Fowler asserting that "an editor should have a pimp for a brother so he'd have someone to look up to."[21] We also find people who gleefully insult their own profession: according to actor Marlon Brando, for example, "an actor's a guy who, if you ain't talking about him, ain't listening,"[22] and according to composer Howard Dietz, "composers shouldn't think too much—it interferes with their plagiarism."[23]

Because they make their living criticizing others, critics are the target of particularly pointed insults. Conductor Sir Thomas Beecham characterizes critics as "drooling, driveling, doleful, depressing, dropsical drips."[24] Author Channing Pollock describes the typical critic as "a legless man who teaches running,"[25] and, pursuing a similar line of insult, author Brendan Behan informs us that "critics are like eunuchs in a harem: They know how it's done, they've seen it done every day, but they're unable to do it themselves."[26]

It is very tempting, when criticized, to respond by abusing those who criticize us. A classic example of such retaliatory abuse is the note that German composer and musician Max Reger, on getting a scathing review of one of his performances, sent to his critic: "I am sitting in the smallest room in my house. I have your review before me. Soon it will be behind me."[27] Before giving in to the temptation to retaliate, though, we should keep in mind that what our critics say might be useful to us if our goal is to excel in some pursuit. Indeed, our critics are generally a more useful source of feedback about our shortcomings than our friends are. We should also keep in mind Stoic philosopher Seneca's advice regarding those who criticize our writing.[28] Before getting angry at these individuals, he says, we should reflect on all the people whose writing we ourselves have criticized. Would we want them to get angry at us and treat us as an enemy? Certainly not! It is inconsistent, then, for us to treat them as enemies. Seneca's conclusion: if you are going to publish, you must be willing to tolerate criticism.

Instead of insulting those who practice certain professions, we can insult those who hold certain beliefs. We might assert, as British humorist J. B. Morton did, that "vegetarians have wicked, shifty eyes and laugh in a cold, calculating manner. They pinch little children, steal stamps, drink water, favor beards."[29] (Although Morton presumably wrote this in jest, it is nevertheless a comment that vegetarians are unlikely to appreciate.) Or we might insult people for their political beliefs. We might agree with philosopher John Stuart Mill that "conservatives are not necessarily stupid, but most stupid people are conservatives"[30] or with author Malcolm Bradbury that "if God had been a liberal, we wouldn't have had the Ten Commandments—we'd have the Ten Suggestions."[31] We also might insult those who believe in a certain religion—which, as author Salman Rushdie found out, can be a dangerous thing to do. In his novel *The Satanic Verses*, Rushdie called into question the extent to which the Quran is divinely inspired. Some Muslims took this to be a profound insult of Islam, and Rushdie found himself subject to a fatwa—an order, issued by Muslim Ayatollah Ruhollah Khomeini, that he be killed.

Some of the most vicious group insults are directed at those of a certain race or those with certain sexual preferences. In uttering such insults, many argue, we cross an important line: our utterances will count not merely as insults, but as hate speech. Those who draw this line advocate that society should intervene to prevent such insults from being uttered and to punish those who utter them. In chapter 10 of this book, we will take a closer look at hate speech laws.

I will end this discussion of group insults by considering what might be called *broad-spectrum insults*. The motive of the person offering such insults is to offend a large but somewhat indeterminate group of people. Consider, by way of illustration, the motives of the driver who had a vanity license plate imprinted with the word *FUGUE*. It could be that this driver is a fan of classical music. It is also possible—indeed, likely—that this driver realized that most of those who saw the plate would be musically illiterate and, on trying to sound out the plate (fug-u), would realize that they had been subjected to what used to be considered the mother of all obscenities. The group "targeted" by this insult, it should be noted, includes everyone who has the misfortune of driving behind this individual.

Sometimes people use t-shirts to inflict broad-spectrum insults on innocent bystanders. It is possible, for example, to buy a t-shirt that says, "Your favorite band sucks." Wearing it would presumably insult everyone who has a favorite band—would, in other words, insult most people. And if this insult isn't broad enough for your tastes, you can purchase a t-shirt that announces, quite simply, that "People suck."

SOMEONE WHO HAS BEEN INSULTED won't necessarily know who insulted him. It is possible, for example, to insult someone by sending him an unsigned letter. Anonymous insults have the advantage of inflicting pain with little chance of retaliation.

One way to increase the pain caused by an insult is to inflict it in public: it is one thing for your boss to call you incompetent behind closed doors; it is quite another for him to call you incompetent over the office loudspeaker system. And if we want to inflict a maximally painful insult with minimal chance of retaliation, we can insult someone in a manner that is simultaneously public and anonymous. Someone can, for example, write a disparaging remark about a coworker on the wall of a toilet stall in the restroom that he and his coworkers share.

Sometimes people are oblivious to the fact that they have been insulted, for the simple reason that the insult was delivered, as we say, "behind their back." An insult can literally be behind someone's back: a child might stick out her tongue at her father when his back is turned. More often, though, a behind-the-back insult will consist of words spoken to someone other than the target of the insult and will be delivered when that person is absent. We have a wonderful name for this activity: *backbiting*.

We backbite people we dislike. Why not insult them to their face? In part because a direct insult runs the risk of retaliation but also because by saying insulting things about them *to other people*, we can perhaps persuade these other people to join us in disliking them.

We also backbite people we regard as social threats. Along these lines, suppose that Alice and Betty are friends but that Betty is becoming increasingly friendly with Carol. If Alice feels threatened by this friendship, she might backbite Carol to Betty in an attempt to prevent the friendship from blossoming any further.

When Alice backbites Carol, she will carefully observe how Betty responds to the backbiting. If Betty joins in the backbiting, Alice will feel relieved; it is a sign that Betty prefers her friendship over that of Carol. But if Betty instead defends Carol against Alice's backbites, Alice will feel more threatened than ever. Not only might she lose Betty's friendship, but there is a chance that Betty will tell Carol about the backbiting, in which case Carol is likely to become a bitter enemy. And even if Betty doesn't ever tell Carol about the insult, she can threaten to do so; she can, in other words, engage in a form of social blackmail.

This discussion of backbiting raises an interesting semantic question: if you don't know you have been insulted, does it count as an insult? I think that *private* behind-the-back insults—such as my sticking my tongue out at you when your back is turned and no one else is present to witness the insult—do not count as insults, any more than an unexpressed critical thought will count as an insult. There is reason to think, though, that *public* behind-the-back insults—such as my sticking my tongue out at you when your back is turned but others can see what I am doing, or my making disparaging remarks about you to others when you aren't around—should count as insults. It may be true that you don't know what took place behind your back and therefore cannot be hurt directly by it, but you can be hurt in an indirect manner. Behind-the-back remarks can, after all, affect someone's social standing and thereby cause him harm.

So far, all the insults we have considered have had humans as their targets. Is it possible, one might wonder, for a nonhuman to be the target of an insult? We might think it is. Suppose, for example, that I make disparaging remarks about a novel: "This book might be useful as material for a compost heap, but as reading material it is utterly worthless." In such cases, it may look like I am insulting the novel, but this appearance is misleading: inasmuch as the novel can't have its feelings hurt by what I say, it will be impossible for me to insult it. I can, however, hurt *people's* feelings by saying these things about the novel—the feelings, for example, of the novelist or the person in the book club who recommended that we read it. Thus, although the novel itself cannot be insulted, it can be used as an instrument with which to insult people.

What about things that, though nonhuman, are animate? What about dogs, for example? Is it possible to insult a dog? I think so. Suppose that the owner of a dog plays a practical joke on it by putting hot sauce on its customary food. This action will presumably displease the dog and as a result it might be said to count as an insult, in some broad sense of the word.

Some will reject this contention: they will argue that dogs simply aren't smart or feeling enough to be insulted. But regardless of whether people can insult dogs, I am convinced that it is possible for dogs to insult people. Suppose, for example, that a dog prefers to sit on the lap of a houseguest rather than on his owner's lap. The owner's feelings might be hurt by this apparent betrayal. Indeed, he might even respond to the dog's "insult" of him by heaping invective on the poor creature.

In this case, some would argue that since the dog did not intend to insult his master—dogs not being sufficiently intelligent to have intentions this complex—the actions of the dog cannot count as an insult. I would respond by pointing out that whether something counts as an insult does not depend on the intentions of the source of the insult. It is, after all, possible to insult someone inadvertently; indeed, even though you are trying very hard not to insult someone, you might nevertheless give him offense. Since the master felt insulted by his dog's behavior, the dog can in some sense be said to have insulted his master.

Given that dogs can insult people, we might wonder whether inanimate things can. Consider again, for example, the computer, somewhere on the Internet, that labeled me a "gorbellied elf-skinned lewdster." Would this be an example of an inanimate thing insulting a person? I think not. For one thing, I found the remark to be curiously inoffensive, in large part because I knew that no one—not even a dog—was responsible for it. To be sure, some person was responsible for the software that generated the remark, but this person, I felt confident, bore no animosity toward me. And besides, this "insult" was in some sense voluntary: I had to go out of my way to get my computer to inflict it on me.

Suppose, by way of contrast, that this same remark appeared on my computer screen as the result of a virus. Suppose, more precisely, that whenever I turned on my computer, the screen labeled me a "gorbellied elf-skinned lewdster." I would not only feel offended but would feel quite angry at whoever was responsible for the virus. Is this a case, then, in which an inanimate object—namely, my computer—insults me? I think not. It is the person who created the virus who is insulting me, albeit anonymously. My computer is merely the vehicle by which the insult is delivered. Along similar lines, when we say that someone sent us an insulting letter, what we are really saying is that they used a letter to insult us.

One last thought on nonhumans as authors of insults. Suppose that intelligent beings exist elsewhere in the universe. Suppose they come to visit us and, after a time, their leader is overheard making the following remark: "Humans are pretty clever for a carbon-based life form." I, for one, would take umbrage.

IT IS POSSIBLE, AS WE HAVE SEEN, to insult someone by insulting an object that is connected to him—a novelist's latest novel, for example. This is an example of an *indirect* insult. In other indirect insults, we insult someone by insulting not some*thing* but some*one* connected to him. Instead of telling him that *he* is fat, ugly, and stupid, we can tell him that *his mother* has these traits, or that his long-dead ancestors have these traits. It may not be possible to insult a dead person—they are, after all, incapable of experiencing displeasure—but this does not stop us from using the dead as an instrument by which to insult the living.

Curiously, indirect insults can be more potent than their direct counterparts. French soccer player Zinedine Zidane was apparently impervious to other players' direct insults of him, but he could not abide having another player insult him indirectly by making a disrespectful remark about his female relatives in a 2006 World Cup match. He head-butted that player and thereby gained international notoriety.[32]

IN THIS CHAPTER, WE HAVE CONSIDERED insults that can best be described as blatant, but it turns out that these insults, although important, represent the visible tip of the insult iceberg. Indeed, unless adults are in unusual circumstances, these insults will play a fairly insignificant role in their daily lives. They will instead find themselves dealing with a variety of subtle insults. It is for this reason that, in the next chapter, we will turn our attention to subtle social digs.

CHAPTER 3

Subtle Digs

IN THE PREVIOUS CHAPTER, we discussed insults that, like daggers, are quick and brutal. Other insults are rather more subtle. When we use one of these subtle insults, there is no flash of steel; indeed, to bystanders who witness the insult, it might look as if nothing at all has happened. Nevertheless, these insults, as we shall see, can be as deadly as their more blatant counterparts.

One of the more insidious weapons in the arsenal of invective is the *insult by omission*. In a typical insult, a person is insulted by what we say or do. In an insult by omission, it isn't what we say or do that insults, it's what we fail to say or do. Suppose, by way of illustration, that you are invited to a dinner party. At this party, you can insult your host by failing to try one of the items she serves for dinner; by trying it but failing to say you like it; by trying it and saying you like it, but failing to have a second helping; or by trying it, saying you like it, and having a second helping, but failing to ask for the recipe. When you leave the party in question, you can insult the host once again by failing to thank her. And even if you do thank her, you can insult her by failing to reciprocate the invitation in a timely fashion. Not all hosts, to be sure, will be sensitive to these sorts of omissions, but some will, and they might exact revenge by never again inviting you to a party.

You can also insult someone by omission by failing to thank him for a gift, and even if you do thank him, you can insult him by failing to appreciate the gift in question. Along these lines, George Bernard Shaw found, in a used-book store, a copy of a book he had given to a friend. The book was inscribed, "With esteem, George Bernard Shaw." He bought the book and sent it to the friend, after making a slight addition to the inscription: "With renewed esteem, George Bernard Shaw."[1]

You can also insult someone by failing to realize who he is. Consider, for example, the Navy admiral who was standing outside a hotel when Robert Benchley—a member of the Algonquin Round Table—came along, quite possibly inebriated. Benchley mistook the admiral for the hotel doorman and asked him to hail a taxi. When the admiral expressed his indignation and told him that he was not a doorman but an admiral, Benchley replied, "all right then, get me a battleship."[2]

You can likewise insult someone by failing to include her on a list. Suppose that at a sports awards banquet, you are naming all the people who contributed to the success of a team. If you inadvertently omit a name, the omitted person will conclude that her contribution to the team was not valued, and she will likely feel insulted. This is why any thoughtful person, when providing a list of names of people to be commended, will put in a disclaimer at the end: "And anyone I might inadvertently have left out." Then again, the fact that you inadvertently left someone out is evidence that her contribution was not particularly memorable, and she might nevertheless feel insulted.

Notice, by the way, that even if you remember to include someone on your list, she might take umbrage at where her name appears on that list. She might, for example, think she deserves to be first rather than second or tenth or wherever it was that you listed her. To avoid insulting people in this manner, you can announce, at the beginning of your list, that the names are in alphabetical order or in no particular order. Even this measure, though, won't stop some people from thinking that the names *should have been* in a particular order— more precisely, an order that placed them higher on the list— in which case they will feel insulted.

INSULTS BY OMISSION, we should realize, differ from the insults by refusal we considered in the previous chapter. Failing to thank the host of a dinner party (because, perhaps, we are drunk or thoughtless) and refusing to shake someone's hand (because we revile him) both involve doing nothing. In the first case, though, we don't intend to insult the host; in the second case, we are intentionally doing nothing, in order to make a brutal social point.

People tend to be sensitive to how other people respond to the social overtures they extend. As a result, someone's failing to respond to an overture can trigger considerable anxiety in the person who extended it. Suppose, by way of illustration, that you give a dinner party, and someone you invited not only doesn't attend but fails to call with an explanation. Why, you will wonder, was he absent? You might, on the morning after the party, do some investigating. You might, to begin with, call people who know the absentee and ask about him. Or you might call the absentee and say something open ended, such as, "we missed you at the party last night."

In making these calls, you are hoping that someone will say something to excuse the absence. You will be relieved, for example, if a friend of the absentee responds to your inquiries by saying, "didn't you hear? He ran into a deer on the way to your party. He totaled his car." Alternatively, you will feel annoyed but not enraged if, when you call the absentee, he tells you that he simply forgot. Your annoyance, by the way, will be somewhat assuaged if, after making this admission, he apologizes profusely and chastises himself for his forgetfulness. But suppose that when you call the absentee and tell him that you missed him at the party, he simply says, "right," with no further attempt at explanation. In this case, you will interpret his absence as an insult by refusal and will therefore feel humiliated and angry. To say the least, it is unlikely that you will invite him to a party again.

ANOTHER INSIDIOUS WEAPON in the arsenal of invective is the *insult by implication*. Suppose, by way of illustration, that a friend discovers that I have been writing poetry, and suppose that a short time later, I hear her tell someone that "Irvine thinks he is a poet." The comment is perfectly true: unless I thought I was in some sense a poet, I wouldn't attempt to write poetry. And yet, the implication in making this comment is that I am deluded in thinking I can write poetry. I will have been insulted by implication, and the insult, rather than being a verbal dagger, is best characterized as a subtle dig.

For another example of an insult by implication, suppose that while we are conversing, I turn away from you abruptly to talk to someone who has walked up, or I stop the conversation to answer my cell phone, or—even worse—I stop the conversation to initiate a cell phone call. The implication is that I value the other person's conversation more than I value yours. Along similar lines, suppose I tell you that I am trying to choose a restaurant to go to (or a movie to see or a book to read), and you give me a recommendation. Suppose that when you later ask what I thought of the restaurant (or movie or book), you discover that I didn't follow your advice. The implication is that I don't value your advice, in which case you might feel insulted by my behavior.

It is also possible to insult someone, by implication, in the process of trying to help her. Suppose, for example, that someone invites you to dinner and that, while watching her cook, you make what you think is a helpful culinary suggestion; she might infer that you are questioning her competence as a cook and might, as a result, feel insulted. Or suppose you hear that a relative is in financial difficulties and offer to lend her some money; she might reply, brusquely, that she doesn't need your charity. You can also insult people by offering to help them lift something (the implication being that they are weak), to help them fix something (the implication being that they aren't handy), or to give them a head start in a race (the implication being that they are slow).

Sometimes those insulted by implication are clever enough not only to recognize the insult but to come up with a reply that also insults by implication. On encountering Theodore Roosevelt in London, for example, Kaiser Wilhelm II invited him to come for a visit the next day: "Be there at two o'clock sharp, for I can only give you forty-five minutes." This, of course, was an insult by implication—the implication being that the kaiser had better things to do with his time than visit with Roosevelt. Roosevelt's reply: "I will be there at two o'clock sharp, but unfortunately I have just twenty minutes to give you."[3]

MANY INSULTS BY IMPLICATION involve an element of comparison: whenever you compare two people, there is a danger that you will offend whoever comes out behind in the comparison. People, after all, don't like being told that someone is better than they are. Indeed, they don't even like being told that someone is as good as they are.

Sometimes the insulting comparison is expressed directly. Consider, for example, the plight of poet Neal Bowers, who in the early 1990s was the victim of a serial plagiarist. The word-thief in question would take Bowers's poems, alter them slightly, and then publish them under his own name. When Bowers showed copies of his poems and the altered versions to friends, he imagined that they would sympathize with him. One friend, rather than showing sympathy, had malicious fun at Bowers's expense: he declared that the changes the plagiarist made to Bowers's poems had, if anything, improved them, the implication being that the plagiarist was a better poet than Bowers.[4]

In other cases, an insulting comparison is merely implied. We already encountered this phenomenon in our discussion of the way people care about where their names appear in lists. Along similar lines, parents experience the pain of comparison when their child announces that he wants to play with his friends rather than playing with his mom and dad, the implication being that he prefers their company to his parents' company. And children experience the pain of comparison when they are the last one to be picked when sides are being chosen in a physical education class. Notice that whoever picked them last probably was not out to insult them; he only wanted to form the best team possible. But to the person picked last, it will feel like an insult.

Sometimes people have the presence of mind, when insulted by an implied comparison, to turn the comparison to their own advantage. Actress Ina Claire (1893–1985) was married to movie star John Gilbert. During an interview, a reporter asked Claire how it felt being married to a celebrity. Her response: "I don't know. Why don't you ask my husband?"[5]

Even if someone comes out ahead in a comparison, he might feel insulted by it. Suppose, for example, that Sam, who is normally a good student, has a bad day and scores poorly on an exam. Suppose his teacher, to chastise him, points out, before the entire class, that "even Tom got a higher grade than Sam did." The teacher might imagine that Tom, who is not a very good student, will be delighted to have the class hear that he outscored Sam. More likely, though, Tom will not enjoy being used as the teacher's benchmark for poor academic performance, and his feelings will be hurt. The insult, in other words, will have caused "collateral damage": it was aimed at Sam but hit Tom as well.

IN THE PREVIOUS CHAPTER, WE EXPLORED the social phenomenon known as backbiting, in which we blatantly insult someone who isn't present. We saw that sometimes the person who is witness to backbiting will report it to the target of the backbiting. Thus, suppose Alice has been saying mean things about Carol to Betty. Betty might subsequently report Alice's comments to Carol. Betty might have benevolent motives for doing this: she might want to warn Carol that Alice is not to be trusted. She might instead have malicious motives, though. In particular, she might want to hurt Carol. By telling her what Alice has said, Betty can inflict the pain of an insult without herself being the author of the insult.

I shall refer to this sort of insult as a *secondhand insult*. The pain caused by a secondhand insult is very real, but its subtlety might make us fail to recognize it for what it is. Indeed, Betty might not even fully understand her motives for reporting Alice's insults to Carol.

Secondhand insults can be quite cunning. Suppose, for example, that a friend calls to ask what you plan to wear to the party Smith is giving. You reply that you didn't know Smith was giving a party. Then it dawns on you, painfully, that you have not been invited to Smith's party. If Smith has always invited you to his parties in the past, you might be insulted (by omission) by his failure to do so on this occasion.

Your friend's behavior could be perfectly innocent: she might have assumed, incorrectly, that you were invited to the party. Then again, she might have known full well that you were not invited and might have taken this opportunity to reveal to you that she is more highly esteemed by the party-giver than you are. In this case, her comments can best be understood as an act of veiled cruelty: she is rubbing in your face the fact that you weren't invited. The effect is the same as coming up and saying, "Ha ha! I was invited to the party and you weren't! Smith likes me better than you!" but without saying any such thing. Indeed, after conveying the insult to you, the friend has a perfect cover for her behavior: "Oh, dear! I'm sorry! I was sure you had been invited! I can't imagine why Smith didn't invite you." The insult, in other words, has what CIA operatives refer to as *plausible deniability*.

Here is another, even more malicious way to inflict this secondhand insult. Rather than talking to you before Smith's party, your friend waits until after the party, at which time she invites you and some other friends—all of whom had attended the party—to lunch. Over dessert, she blurts out, "Wasn't that a great party?" In this case, your friend not only wants you to discover that you were not invited to the party but wants you to make this discovery in the presence of an audience that can watch your anguished reaction.

What if we want to inflict the pain of a secondhand insult, but no one has provided us with an insult to report? In this case, we can simply fabricate the insult. Betty, for example, might tell Carol that Alice says she is anorexic, even though Alice has said no such thing. If Carol is sufficiently insulted, she will stop talking to Alice and will thereby deprive herself of the opportunity to discover the truth of the matter.

I will give entertainer Oscar Levant the final word on sec-ondhand insults: "I never read bad reviews about myself be-cause my best friends invariably tell me about them."[6]

IT IS POSSIBLE, as we have seen, to insult someone without in-tending to do so. Sometimes, the person we accidentally insult will assume that our insult was malicious. In other cases, though, she will realize that we didn't intend to insult her. We might think this realization would take away much or even all of the sting of the insult, and in some cases it will. In other cases, though, having someone realize that we didn't intend to insult her will make the insult that much more painful.

Allow me to illustrate. I was at a gathering at which a man, talking about his own children, said he hoped they wouldn't marry someone from a broken family, the implication being that doing this would decrease the chance of their having a long, happy marriage. He did not know it, but one of the people he was talking to was a divorced mother, meaning that her children were the sort of children he wouldn't want his own children to marry. The woman said nothing in reply, but the remark visibly pained her.

If the man had come up to her and said, "I wouldn't want my kids to marry your kids. I would fear that your kids' mar-riages would end, like yours did, in divorce," she might have found his remark to be painful and embarrassing. She could, however, have told herself that the man wasn't very nice to have said this and that he was obviously out to ruin her day. These thoughts could have helped her dismiss the insult as being the prattle of a mean-spirited individual. But because he didn't know she was divorced—because the insult was inadvertent—it will be hard for her to dismiss it in this manner. In expressing his views, the man wasn't trying to make her feel bad; instead, he was explaining, in a sincere manner, how he felt. By doing so, however, he was accidentally revealing to her something that he wouldn't want her to know.

There is a curious phrase we use to describe this man's behavior: we say that he put his foot in his mouth. In the incident just described, the man did not realize what he had done, but if someone, after he made his remark, had told him that the woman he was talking to was divorced—or if she herself had announced the fact—it is likely that he would have felt acute embarrassment: it would have pained him to have, through his thoughtlessness, unintentionally caused her pain.

To avoid putting our foot in our mouth, we must, when engaged in casual conversation, be very careful about what we say, especially if we are talking to someone we don't know well. We should avoid referring, for example, to "those pin-headed liberals," and we should avoid belittling adults who still live with their parents, since for all we know, the person we are talking to is a liberal who lives with his mother. Conversation can be a minefield of unintended insults, and a good conversationalist will take care to avoid stepping on any. He will take to heart the admonition, attributed to Oscar Wilde, that "a gentleman never insults anyone unintentionally."[7]

And when we are talking to someone, we need to worry about unintentionally insulting not only him but anyone else who might be eavesdropping on our conversation. One might expect an eavesdropper, if stung by what we say, to remain silent rather than admit to eavesdropping. It is my experience, though, that this is not the case. In one incident, an eavesdropper made it abundantly clear to me how much my remarks—the ones I made to someone else in what I thought was a private conversation—had hurt her. Significantly, I did not respond to her remarks by scolding her for eavesdropping; I was too mortified to do anything but sit in stunned silence.

Suppose that instead of uttering our critical remarks about someone, we record them in a diary. Suppose he finds the diary and, without our permission, reads it. Our remarks will probably cause him considerable pain, since he will know that this is what we really think of him. The pain might be sufficient to make him confront us regarding our comments, even though to do so, he will have to admit that he snooped into our diary.

BECAUSE POLITE PEOPLE endeavor to avoid insulting others, even unintentionally, it is possible to use insults as a weapon, not by inflicting one but by claiming to have been the target of one. Suppose, for example, you want to buy a house, the asking price of which is $500,000. Suppose you think this price is ridiculously high and make an offer of $350,000. The real estate agent, after conferring with her clients, might tell you that they not only reject your offer but that, quite frankly, they find it insulting.

In this case, it is unlikely that the sellers were in fact insulted by your offer; it is unlikely, in particular, that they burst into tears on hearing the offer or shouted out, "That potential buyer has impugned my honor! Vengeance will be mine!" Why, then, did the agent tell you that they were offended? Perhaps she has a penchant for hyperbole. Alternatively, her comment might be part of a socially shrewd negotiating tactic. She had hoped that on hearing that you had insulted the sellers, your social instincts would be triggered. More precisely, you would feel embarrassed and take steps to remedy the situation, and what better way to do this than by raising your offer?

Besides manipulating people by claiming, falsely, that someone else was offended by their behavior, we can manipulate them by claiming, again falsely, that *we ourselves* were offended. Suppose, for example, that I didn't want to go to the party you were giving; indeed, had you invited me, I would have declined the invitation. I might nevertheless tell you that I was deeply hurt by your failure to invite me. If by means of this ploy I can make you feel guilty, I might be able to get you to do things for me that you otherwise wouldn't do.

For another example of using "fraudulent insults" as a weapon, we can turn to America's college campuses. In classrooms, the content of discussions is often determined by the most sensitive student present. All it takes is for one person to announce that she is upset by what is being said, and the discussion will quickly and apologetically be redirected. It used to be that family gatherings were where you had to watch what you said—you didn't want to upset your Aunt Bertha, after all—and college was where you were free to speak your mind. Now the situation is reversed: college campuses are where you have to watch what you say, lest someone takes offense.

In some cases, one suspects that the hypersensitive students I have described are only feigning umbrage. They might do this in a last-ditch attempt to avoid losing an argument: "Stop!

You are hurting my feelings!" Or maybe they think that this is how they can best contribute to classroom discussion—by making sure that it remains "politically correct." And if their umbrage is in fact sincere, we can meaningfully ask whether their sensitivity came to them naturally or whether it was something someone taught them to experience. I will have more to say about this state of affairs in chapter 10.

CHAPTER 4

Bludgeoned with Praise

PRAISE CAN TAKE many forms. We can praise someone overtly by complimenting her—by telling her, for example, how much we like her new hairdo. After someone gives a musical performance, we might applaud, give them a standing ovation, or yell "Bravo!" Praise can also be subtle. In the same way, for example, as we can insult someone by implication, we can praise him by implication: a woman might tell a man how lucky his girlfriend is. Likewise, one of the highest forms of praise is to emulate someone.

Sometimes, words of praise directed at another person are less generous than they seem. In particular, in praising someone else, we might in fact be praising ourselves. Thus, when a teacher praises the accomplishments of a pupil, she is indirectly praising herself: had it not been for her teaching ability, this pupil would not have gone as far as he did. When parents praise their child's beautiful eyes, they are indirectly boasting about their own genetic makeup. And when a man tells his wife how beautiful she is, he is in part complimenting himself on his ability to attract and retain a beautiful woman.

EVEN THOUGH PRAISE is the opposite of insults, it is possible to insult someone by attempting to praise him. Suppose, for example, that a baseball coach tells one of his players that he is the best outfielder on the team. This is high praise, unless the player already takes it for granted that he is the best outfielder on the team and imagines himself to be the best outfielder in the whole league. And if the player fancies himself to be a better pitcher than outfielder, he might be offended that the coach praises his fielding but not his pitching.

It is also possible to insult someone by praising his past accomplishments. Such praise, after all, implies that his greatest accomplishments are behind him. This might happen if, after being introduced to an actor, we rave about his early movies but fail to mention those that followed. In this case, we probably don't intend to make the actor feel bad, but we might nevertheless ruin his day.

Sometimes, people praise us sincerely but for the wrong reasons, and as a result, we take the praise as an insult. On a teaching evaluation, for instance, one of my students might write: "Professor Irvine is an excellent teacher because he doesn't make us learn stuff." This is an example of what we call a *backhanded* or *left-handed compliment*. The problem is that this student's idea of excellence in a teacher—not making students learn "stuff"—is at odds with my own idea. What he intends as a compliment of my teaching therefore comes across as an insult. Along similar lines, suppose someone with terrible taste in clothes sincerely compliments your outfit. You might, in such cases, prefer that this person, rather than praising your taste, had insulted it: "If *she* likes my outfit, then it must be horrid!"

In the preceding chapter we examined second-hand insults, in which someone reports to us the insulting things someone has said about us. To make these insults even more devious, we can mix in an element of praise. Consider, by way of illustration, the following remark, made to a woman friend: "I don't care what anyone says, you aren't fat." Unless this woman is unusual, she will find that the praise we offer is more than counterbalanced by the information that someone thinks she is overweight; indeed, she might find our "praise" to be quite upsetting.

WE CAN ALSO INSULT someone not by praising him but by praising someone else in his presence. When, for example, a child tells his father that his friend's dad is really smart, the father might take this as an indication that his son thinks he is not particularly smart, and his feelings might be hurt. By the same token, a woman might get upset if her husband praises her sister's figure, and a man might get upset if his wife makes admiring comments about his friend's firm buttocks.

If we praise someone in the presence not of a single person but a crowd of people, we multiply our chance of insulting people by the implied comparison. When a bandleader lavishes praise on one of the band's two trombone players, for example, the other trombone player will likely feel insulted. And even if the band has only one trombone player, the band's flute player might feel somewhat insulted that the bandleader failed to praise her as well: to her way of thinking, she contributes as much to the band's performance as the trombone player does. Similarly, when workers at a meeting hear the boss describe a worker who isn't present as being charming and brilliant, the other employees might react by wondering why this one employee was picked out for praise. Is it because the boss thinks the rest of them *aren't* charming and brilliant?

When you praise someone in public, it is therefore wise to avoid superlatives: if you refer to someone as being "the best," you are likely to insult all those who regard themselves as being at least her equal. It is far safer, when you publicly praise someone, to refer to her as being "*one of* the best." Then, if someone complains, you can tell him that you also regard him as one of the best—which explanation will fail if, instead of thinking he is *one of* the best, he is confident that he is *the* best.

We might, at this point, be tempted to conclude that if we want to avoid offending people, it is a good idea to do our praising in private. Such praise might accidentally offend the person who is the target of our praise, but at least there will be no danger of insulting other people as well. Right? Not necessarily. There is the danger, after all, that the person we praise in private will take it upon herself to report our praise to others. Thus, a trombonist the bandleader has privately praised might tell the band's other trombonist what the bandleader said, and this other trombonist might thereby feel insulted. In this case, I should add, the first trombonist might not have intended to hurt the feelings of the other trombonist; then again, this might have been her prime objective in talking to her bandmate.

These examples should make it clear what a minefield our social interactions can be. It is bad enough that our innocent remarks can be construed as insulting, but even our attempts to praise can give rise to hurt feelings! This is evidence of the extent to which we have been wired, by our evolutionary past, to care about our standing on the social hierarchy. It also shows how important it is, if we want to be able to enjoy our relationships with other people, to devise a strategy to avoid insulting them and to prevent their insults, both intentional and accidental, from ruining our day.

IT IS POSSIBLE, AS WE HAVE SEEN, to insult people by trying to praise them; it is also possible, though, to be insulted by people's reaction to our praise. In particular, if we confer an honor on someone, and she declines that honor, we are likely to take offense.

Along these lines, consider the behavior of eccentric mathematician Grigori Perelman, who in 2002 published a proof of the Poincaré conjecture, one of the most challenging problems in mathematics. The mathematical community subsequently showered him with awards, including the Fields Medal and the Millennium Prize. Perelman responded by unapologetically declining these awards, along with the money—in the case of the Millennium Prize, a cool million dollars—that came with them. By behaving in this way, Perelman offended those who had gone to the trouble of awarding him the honors, since by declining them, he implied that these honors weren't worthy of him. He also offended his fellow mathematicians by making them look foolish for being enamored of such honors.[1]

It isn't clear what Perelman's motives were for declining the honors he was awarded. In the case of the Fields Medal, he appears to have been insulted that other mathematicians were named as corecipients of the prize.[2] One thing that is certain, though, is that if he declined the honors so he could stay out of the spotlight and preserve his privacy, his plan backfired horribly. Once people in general learned of the existence of a man who seemed indifferent to honors and wealth, they became deeply, invasively curious about him. At one point, journalists burst into Perelman's apartment in order to film it. And thanks to the press coverage, Perelman found it difficult to leave his apartment without someone taking his picture.[3]

In chapter 11, we will again turn our attention to honors and how best to behave when awarded them. I will suggest that although we should not pursue honors, if they nevertheless come our way, our best strategy is to quietly, humbly accept them and then carry on with our life as if nothing had happened.

THE MOST COMMON WAY in which people intentionally use praise to insult others is to praise them in a sarcastic manner. Someone on our softball team drops a pop fly that he should have caught: "Nice catch!" we exclaim. Someone locks his keys in his car: "Brilliant!" we comment. Someone has his driver's license revoked because he has too many accidents: we might, with much fanfare, give him a good driver award at our next social gathering.

It is also possible for groups to engage in sarcastic praise. At a concert I attended, for example, the warm-up set was played by a musician the audience didn't particularly like. When the musician had finished his final number and arose to leave the stage, the audience—which had been largely oblivious to the fact that he was playing—startled to attention and spontaneously broke into thunderous but insincere applause. President Bill Clinton met with similar sarcastic praise when, during the 1988 Democratic convention, he gave a speech to nominate Michael Dukakis. The speech was apparently both long and boring: near the end of the speech, Clinton uttered the words "in closing," and the audience cheered heartily.[4]

One interesting subcategory of insincere praise involves intentional ambiguity: we make a comment that can be taken in two ways, one of which is complimentary and the other of which is insulting. Thus, when an aspiring novelist sent a manuscript for British statesman and writer Benjamin Disraeli to critique, he responded as follows: "Thank you for the manuscript. I shall lose no time in reading it."[5] This kind of ambiguous praise differs from the backhanded compliments discussed above. The person offering those compliments sincerely thinks he is complimenting us; in the case of ambiguous praise, by way of contrast, the person intends to insult us.

The possibility of insulting us by praising us sarcastically (or ambiguously) raises an interesting question: if someone wants to insult us, why not just do so? Why, for example, didn't the audience simply boo the musician they didn't like? Why go to all the trouble of giving him an insincere ovation? Likewise, why didn't Disraeli write back that he had no time to waste on the manuscript he had been sent? Or not respond at all, which also would have been insulting to the aspiring novelist?

The answer to these questions, I think, is that sarcastic praise can inflict far more pain than ordinary insults can. Suppose, for example, the musician fails to detect the audience's sarcasm. He struts proudly from the stage, only to have his illusions shattered by those waiting there: "You fool! They didn't like you, they hated you!" Likewise, suppose the aspiring novelist had tried to impress an editor by showing him the note Disraeli had sent. The editor might puncture the novelist's balloon by explaining that he had misconstrued the note: "I think what Mr. Disraeli is telling you is that he is *not* going to read your manuscript, inasmuch as doing so would be a waste of time!" Sarcastic praise creates the possibility that the person praised will take the praise seriously, making him look all the more foolish.

THERE IS ANOTHER WAY to use sarcastic praise to insult someone: we can deliver what might be called an *ambush insult*. Consider, by way of illustration, Groucho Marx's comment to S. J. Perelman: "From the moment I picked up your book until I laid it down I was convulsed with laughter. Someday I intend reading it."[6] Beethoven used this device when he told another composer, "I liked your opera. I think I will set it to music."[7] So did poet Antoine de Rivarol who, when presented with a two-line poem written by another poet, had this to say: "Very nice, although there are dull stretches."[8] For one last example of an ambush insult, consider Oscar Wilde's comment about Frank Harris: He "is invited to all the great houses in England—once."[9] Each of these insults starts out with what sounds like sincere praise, but then the praise transmogrifies, before our very eyes, into a disparaging remark.

Devising ambush insults, like devising ambiguous insults, requires a degree of intelligence on the part of the insulter.

In the early 1990s, though, comedians Mike Myers and Dana Carvey invented what amounts to a generic ambush insult: say words of praise to someone and then, after a brief pause, add "not!" For example, "You are a great tennis player...not!" Fortunately for humanity, this particular form of ambush insult has fallen into disuse.

Ambush insults are effective because most people are starved for praise. As a result, when they hear what sounds like praise, they perk up. Ambush insults exploit this phenomenon. They create in people the expectation that more praise is forthcoming—that someone is about to make their day. This means that when, instead of being lavished with more praise, they are hit with an insult, the emotional plunge is that much further. Thus, the authors of ambush insults praise their targets for the same reason as farmers feed their cattle—namely, to fatten them for the kill.

In one ambush insult variant, we don't praise our target; we instead wait for her to praise herself. Thus, suppose someone whose cooking skills leave much to be desired announces that she thinks herself a pretty good cook. We might respond to this self-praise by emitting a derisive snort. In doing this, we will have caught our target at her moment of maximum vulnerability, and our insult will therefore have much greater impact than if we had simply walked up to her and said that we didn't care for her cooking.

Although ambush insults are often meant in jest, they can also play a central role in what turns out to be a vicious attack. In 2007, one such case made the headlines. In Dardenne Prairie, Missouri, a woman named Lori Drew went on the Internet and presented herself as a teenage boy named Josh. Under this guise, she allegedly contacted Megan Meier, a neighbor and former friend of her daughter. (Megan had apparently insulted this friend—and the friend's mother as well—by breaking off the friendship.) Ms. Drew, who knew that Megan was on anti-depressant medications,[10] had "Josh" flirt with Megan online and say complimentary things. This was the praise. Then came the ambush: without warning, Josh turned on Megan. Among other things, he told her that "Megan Meier is a slut. Megan Meier is fat."[11] Shortly thereafter, Megan committed suicide.

Drew was subsequently tried and found guilty of a misde-meanor in connection with having gained unauthorized access to a MySpace account.[12] The conviction was subsequently overturned.[13]

PEOPLE ARE OFTEN RELUCTANT to praise others. When circum-stances require them to do so, they might offer genuine and sincere praise, but then, almost without realizing what they are doing, they might go on to temper the praise with insults. Suppose, for example, that the business we started in our garage goes on to become such a success that we are the sub-ject of a glowing profile on the front page of *The Wall Street Journal*. A relative might call to congratulate us: "You've gone far in life . . . for someone who never even finished high school." In the process of praising us, this relative is rubbing salt into what for us is probably an old wound—our failure to graduate from high school.

In this case, the person who is praising us seems to be expe-riencing a degree of ambivalence toward our accomplishments and as a result feels the need to temper his praise with a reminder of our shortcomings. Thus, his praise is different from the kind of backhanded compliments we examined earlier in this chapter: in those "compliments," we were confident that the person sincerely intended to praise us. This sort of praise also differs from the ambush insults we have explored: in those cases, we were (eventually) confident that the person's intention in praising us was to insult us. In the case just considered, though, the relative's motives seem curiously mixed. Yes, he wants to praise us, but at the same time, he wants to make sure we stay in our place, socially speaking. I should add that the relative himself might not fully understand his motives for doing what he did.

People mix praise with insults in this manner, I think, because they feel vaguely threatened by the successes of others: they imagine that someone else's success somehow diminishes their own. They know that they are expected to congratulate friends, relatives, and coworkers who succeed in some undertaking, but in the process of doing so, they feel compelled to downplay the significance of those accomplishments and thereby maintain the significance of their own. People also worry, I suspect, that if they offer someone undiluted praise, they will lose their position on the social hierarchy. By following their praise for someone with a put-down, people prevent this from happening: "You did well, but it doesn't mean that you are better than I am."

ONE PARTICULARLY VICIOUS FORM of sarcastic praise involves undertaking a campaign of flattery: over an extended period of time, we repeatedly praise someone we in fact despise. Taking this strategy one step further, we can join with others to flatter someone: we can, in other words, enter into a conspiracy of flattery.

Sometimes these conspiracies are meant to humiliate their target. I remember, for example, an incident in junior high. A girl who wasn't particularly popular showed up one day wearing a scarf. The other girls, who themselves abhorred scarves, started praising it sarcastically. The scarf-wearer failed to detect their sarcasm and responded to their praise by buying and wearing more scarves, which only intensified the praise showered on her by those involved in the conspiracy. It finally dawned on the poor girl that she had been set up. This was, to be sure, a cruel trick to play on her, and the conspirators who played it not only realized that it was cruel but reveled in its very cruelty.

People in positions of authority are particularly susceptible to campaigns of flattery. Suppose, for example, that workers despise their boss. If they tell him so, they will be fired. If, however, they make him the target of a campaign of flattery, they can benefit in two ways. First, a boss who has been buttered up with flattery will be more likely to promote them or give them a pay raise. Second, even if they never get a promotion or pay raise, a campaign of flattery, carried on by a group of disgruntled employees, has considerable entertainment value. Thus, at the water cooler, we might find one employee boasting about her latest accomplishment: "The other day, I told the boss that I had learned more from him than from all my other bosses combined, and—can you believe it?—he responded by telling me that lots of workers have told him this! He says that his most important contribution to the company is in playing the role of mentor. This guy is so clueless! What an idiot!"

The time might come when a workplace campaign of flattery can safely be revealed to the boss. Suppose, for example, that the boss is ignominiously fired. On his way out of the building, employees, if they are sufficiently spiteful, might line up to tell him what a fool he is for having believed their praise. Or, if they encounter the boss after they retire, they might reveal the conspiracy they engaged in: "We all hated you!" This comment is likely to set off a bout of soul searching on the part of the boss. "Which of the other things that people told me," he will wonder, "were insincere?"

THE GENIUS—the cruel genius—of conspiracies of flattery is the manner in which they exploit human weakness. We are, as Greek essayist Plutarch noted two millennia ago, exquisitely susceptible to flattery: "It is because of . . . self-love that everybody is himself his own foremost and greatest flatterer, and hence finds no difficulty in admitting the outsider to witness with him and to confirm his own conceits and desires."[14] In using flattery to insult us, our enemies exploit this self-love.

People typically initiate a conspiracy of flattery against someone because they think he has a character flaw: they might, for example, think he is both conceited and thickheaded. Rather than directly insulting him, they trick him into demonstrating the truth of the accusation: if he fails to detect the conspiracy of flattery, it will become apparent to everyone—except to him—exactly how conceited and thickheaded he is. Thus, conspiracies of flattery have something in common with practical jokes. In a good practical joke, we create a situation in which the victim of the joke will demonstrate a character flaw: we might, as we have seen, glue a dime to the floor so we can watch the office tightwad try to pick it up. In a conspiracy of flattery, we don't do anything "practical," we just slather on praise.

Conspiracies of flattery can backfire. Consider again the boss whose employees continually flatter him. As this boss becomes more and more convinced of his brilliance, he might lose touch with reality, and this can create a perilous environment for his flatterers: rather than being amused by his actions, they might be horrified as he makes decisions that threaten the future profitability of the company and thereby put their jobs in jeopardy. It will be very difficult, at this late stage, to save the boss from himself.

Plutarch recognized this danger. "An ugly man," he wrote, "who is made to believe that he is handsome, or a short man that he is tall, is not for long a party to the deception, and the injury that he suffers is slight and not irremediable." This cannot be said, though, of praise "which accustoms a man to treat vices as virtues, so that he feels not disgusted with them but delighted, which also takes away all shame for his errors." It was this kind of praise, he says, that brought afflictions upon the people of Sicily, that ruined Egypt, and that ruined the character of the Romans.[15]

One periodically encounters a person who, because of the position he holds, has over the course of years or decades been the unwitting victim of overlapping conspiracies of flattery. Such individuals are convinced of their own value to humanity.

Even though they have just met you, they imagine that you, too, will want to praise them, and until you do, they will entertain you with tales that reveal just how wonderful they are. Pity anyone who has to sit next to this sort of person on a transcontinental flight.

THOUGHTFUL PEOPLE will think twice before basking in whatever praise comes their way. It could well be, after all, that the praise is insincere and the person who seems to be praising them is in fact insulting them. The praise in question might, for example, be sarcastic or ambiguous, it might be the prelude to an ambush insult, or it might be part of a campaign of flattery. Those who have power over others—including bosses, teachers, and military officers—need to be particularly hesitant to take at face value whatever praise their subordinates direct toward them.

Because thoughtful people worry about falling victim to insincere praise, they go through life with their sarcasm detector turned on. Sometimes, a detector is so sensitive that a person will reject all praise out of hand: offer sincere praise to such an individual, and he is likely to respond not with gratitude but with an insult. Thus, Oscar Wilde, after falling victim to a clever repartee by James Whistler, responded, quite sincerely, by saying, "I wish I had said that!" Rather than accepting this as a compliment and thanking Wilde, Whistler replied, "You will, Oscar, you will!"[16]

CHAPTER 5

Benign Insults

I WAS AT A GATHERING when a friend, who knew I am an author, asked me if I was working on a book. I answered that I was—a book on insults. We then worked our way through what turned out to be the common misconceptions about this project: "No," I explained, "it is not a book *of* insults, it is a book *about* insults."

"What about them?" he asked.

In response to this question, I started telling him about the role insults play in social relationships. He remained puzzled. "Isn't it pretty rare," he asked, "for a person to insult someone, particularly if they are adults?"

I went on to explain that although direct, confrontational insults are indeed rare, subtle insults are commonplace. I was starting to describe the forms these subtle insults can take when a member of our gathering, beloved by us all, announced that he was leaving because he had another social engagement to attend. This announcement was greeted by a chorus of catcalls.

"What, we're not good enough for a social climber like yourself?"

"Good riddance!"

"He's probably headed to a strip joint."

And in response to this last insult, the departing person shot back, "Compared to you yahoos, the clientele of a strip joint would seem pretty classy."

When the hubbub subsided, I turned back to the person with whom I was conversing: "There you have it," I said. "Four solid insults in the space of ten seconds. They are far more common than most people think."

"But those weren't really insults," he replied. "They were just teasing him, and he in turn was teasing them back."

WERE READERS TO KEEP an insult journal in which they recorded the insults directed at them in a typical week, along with the sources of those insults, they would make an interesting discovery. If a reader is seven years old, she might end up with pages and pages in which other kids call her, say, stupid or a pooh-pooh head. If the reader is an adult, though, she will only rarely be the target of a spiteful insult. What she will find, to the contrary, is that the vast majority of insults directed at her are benign and that they have friends and relatives as their source. She will find, in other words, that most of the insults she encounters are part of the social phenomenon known as teasing.

Before we proceed with this discussion of teasing, it is important to distinguish between teasing that is playful and teasing that is malicious. Malicious teasing can cause considerable suffering in its target; playful teasing, by way of contrast, can trigger delight. Not only that, but playful teasing, as we shall see, can play an important role in helping us maintain relationships.

If we visit a playground, we might encounter instances of malicious teasing. A bunch of children, for example, might have formed a circle around a particular child, and they might all be yelling that he is fat. They do this because they want to cause their victim anguish. Or, rather than a bunch of children maliciously teasing one child, it might be a single child—a bully—who makes a point of maliciously teasing other children. People bully others for a number of reasons.[1] They might, to begin with, bully someone because they dislike or envy him. Alternatively, they might bully someone simply because they are in a bad mood or because they are bored and want to entertain themselves. And although they might not consciously realize as much, many bullies bully because they want to enhance their social status: groups typically have a dominance hierarchy, and by bullying others, it is possible to ascend that hierarchy. Bullying also promotes conformity within a group: those who depart from what the bully takes to be proper group norms—say, by dressing or acting differently—are punished for doing so.

Children who are the targets of bullying typically experience embarrassment and anger, and the pain the bullying causes them can last for decades.[2] It is curious, but adults, who themselves would not hesitate to call the police if someone bullied them, are often reluctant to intervene to stop bullying on the playground. As a result, children sometimes take matters into their own hands: after being bullied for years, they mentally snap and strike back violently at those who bullied them. Students who shoot up their schools often claim that they are doing it in part as a result of having been bullied.[3]

PLAYFUL TEASING and malicious teasing both involve insults. The insults involved in playful teasing, though, are not intended to inflict pain on their target. In the case I described, for example, we insulted the individual who was leaving our party because we like him and want him to like us in turn. If this seems paradoxical, welcome to the strange world of interpersonal relationships!

Here are some other examples of playful teasing. The parents of a child who is always forgetting things might tease him by saying—as my parents used to—that he would forget his head if it weren't attached by his neck. Parents whose child is eating them out of house and home might tease him by calling him *Horse*. A wife who catches her husband eying a curvaceous young woman might tell him that he is delusional if he thinks this woman would give a geezer like him the time of day. A person might introduce a friend who is notable for—and is in fact proud of—her promiscuity as being a person who loves mankind...one man at a time. A boss might, when an employee walks into a meeting late, playfully interrogate her: "Let me guess: you were abducted by aliens on the way to work. That would, by my count, be the third abduction this month."

Sometimes when we playfully tease someone, the person takes offense at what we say. In such cases, we typically respond by explaining that what we said—the utterance that under normal circumstances would clearly count as an insult—wasn't intended as an insult. To the contrary, we were simply joshing, kidding, ribbing, or razzing the target of our teasing. Or, colloquially, we might tell him not to get all in a huff—that we were just pulling his chain, rattling his cage, or funning him. Likewise, if someone's feelings are hurt after we tell a joke at his expense, we might explain that we weren't laughing *at* him, we were laughing *with* him.

Suppose the teased person remains offended. The person who teased him might now become critical: "Can't you take a joke?" And if it turns out that the teased person can't take a joke, it will affect his relationship with the joker in question. The joker will start handling the other person with, as the expression goes, kid gloves, and the relationship between them is unlikely to be as close as it would be if the person were tolerant of playful teasing—if, that is, he happily let friends and relatives verbally abuse him.

We can locate our various relationships on a continuum, according to the role teasing plays in them. At one end of this continuum, we find relationships in which teasing plays no part at all. If, for example, we have an uncle who, besides being elderly and solemn, lacks a sense of humor, we would be foolish to tease him—unless it is our goal to be written out of his will. At the other end of the continuum we find what are sometimes called *joking relationships*. In such relationships, explains social anthropologist Alfred Radcliffe-Brown, one person is required to tease the other, who in turn is required to take no offense at being teased or, better still, to tease back.[4] If one party in such a relationship momentarily gets serious, the other party might find the behavior to be at first perplexing and then unsettling. Most of our relationships lie in the middle part of the teasing continuum, though, and a particular relationship can move around on the continuum, depending on how close or distant the relationship becomes.

TEASING OF THE PLAYFUL SORT is ubiquitous.[5] Nearly everyone teases, including babies less than one year old. Their teasing, to be sure, is not verbal; it is instead physical. A baby might offer something to a parent, for example, only to withdraw it when the parent reaches for it. When they do this, says psychologist Vasudevi Reddy, babies are playing a role similar to that played by circus clowns: they are "taking serious intentions and agreed meanings and turning them round, playing with their limits, and challenging their incorporation into shared culture."[6]

We tease for any number of reasons. To begin with, we tease friends, relatives, neighbors, and coworkers to remind them of their foibles: in our teasing we point out, in a non-threatening manner, what we take to be their shortcomings and character flaws. Consider again the boss who asked whether his tardy employee had been abducted by aliens. The boss was annoyed by the employee's tendency to show up late. He could have expressed this annoyance with a threat: "Our company has a policy against tardiness. You have violated this policy three times this month. Get here on time, or you will be terminated." Doing this, however, would have alienated the employee. It is because the employer likes and values the employee and wants to remain on good terms with her that he resorts to teasing. By doing this, he can (hopefully) get his point across, and the employee will mend her ways without coming to resent her boss.

Whenever two people spend lots of time together, they make an interesting discovery: behaviors that might have been fascinating or even cute when first encountered can become quite annoying on their hundredth repetition. Teasing is one of the best ways to deal with the issues that arise in a long-term relationship. Suppose, for example, that a wife is unhappy about how messy her husband's home office is. She can nag him, chide him for his messiness, or even present him with an ultimatum, but this is likely to antagonize him. Alternatively, she can playfully tease him about the things he does that irritate her: "Someday, I'm going to hear muffled cries for help coming from your office, darling, and it will turn out that you have been buried in an avalanche of papers and books. Maybe then you will do something about this horrid mess... if you are able."

There is no guarantee, of course, that teasing someone will bring about changes in his behavior. Nevertheless, in many cases it is a more effective and pleasant way to bring about such changes than nagging or scolding. Furthermore, even if teasing has zero impact on someone's annoying behavior, it at least gives the annoyed person a chance to vent.

Couples instinctively understand the value of teasing, and so they set about mocking each other's habits, preferences, mannerisms, or speech patterns. They make fun of each other's bodies. They give each other pet names that are loosely based on what they perceive to be their partner's shortcomings. The woman who disliked the disorderly state of her husband's office, for example, might lovingly refer to him as Rat—short for Pack Rat.

Sometimes those who feel compelled to playfully tease someone worry that he will instead take it as a rebuke. In these cases, they will do something to indicate that a tease is intended. The above-mentioned wife, for example, might preface her insult with a declaration of affection: "You know I love you, Rat, but your office is a God-awful pig sty. Why do you choose to live like a pig?" (And she might follow this declaration by emitting a few "oink-oink" noises.)

In an ideal relationship, teasing would be unnecessary: those in the relationship would either accept each other just as they are or, failing that, would graciously accede to each other's requests that they change. In most real-world relationships, though, teasing plays an important role: it allows one partner to bring up sensitive issues in a manner that, she hopes, won't alienate the other partner. If not broached, these issues might undermine the relationship.

It is indeed curious: the same insults that can, under some circumstances, weaken or even destroy a relationship, can, under other circumstances, preserve or strengthen that same relationship.

PEOPLE ALSO TEASE EACH OTHER as a kind of social test. Above I described the insults directed at the person who revealed that he was leaving our party early to attend another social engagement. This information triggered an element of social anxiety in the rest of us: "Has he found friends that he prefers to us?" we wondered. "Are we merely the friends he warms up with until the real party, with his real friends, begins?" In order to allay these anxieties, we tested him with a barrage of insults. Had he taken offense at our insults, it would have been a sign that he thought he was better than we are, and he would therefore have failed the test. We might, as a result, have thought twice about inviting him to future parties. But because he instead responded to our insults with playful counterinsults, we concluded that he regarded himself as being our social equal and therefore that our relationship with him was not in jeopardy.

Here are some other examples of teasing as a kind of social test. Your relatives, on learning that you got a pay raise, might tease you by asking whether in the future a butler will be answering your door. Or your fellow students, on learning that you made the dean's list because of your good grades, might tease you by suggesting that you must have bribed your professors. Such insults, I think, are triggered by a combination of envy and social insecurity. In particular, the insulters worry that because of your success, you have gained social status and will therefore be unwilling, in the future, to accept them as social equals. They tease you to see if there is indeed reason for concern.

If you respond to their teasing in a defensive manner, they might conclude that you do think yourself socially superior to them. Suppose, however, that you respond with a bit of self-deprecating humor. You might, in the first case described, tell your relations that although you don't have any plans to hire a butler to answer your door, you can, with the raise, finally afford to get your doorbell fixed; and in the second case, you might tell your fellow students that professors are easy to bribe—that all it took was twenty-dollar bills stapled to your final exams. By laughing at your own success, you will convince them that success has not gone to your head—that you don't regard yourself as being superior to them and that they therefore shouldn't feel threatened by your success.

People like to belong to groups, in part because they like having the identity that group membership affords them. Once they join a group, though, they typically find that to remain in it, they must conform to group norms. Fail to conform, and the other members of the group might resort to teasing in an attempt to get an errant group member to mend his ways.[7] If this attempt fails, though, the group might jettison the member.

Suppose, for example, that someone who belongs to a group of committed runners announces that he has lately tried cycling and just loves it. His fellow runners will quickly realize that if he starts cycling seriously, it will be detrimental to the group: the runner in question won't be able to train with them and go to races with them. They might, as a result, resort to teasing to talk him back into the fold: "Cycling is for sissies; real men run."

Sometimes, group-membership teasing can be extreme. Thus, according to linguist Koenraad Kuiper, New Zealand rugby players, before and after games and practices, are in the habit of insulting each other, often in a manner that can only be described as profoundly obscene. In one relatively tame insult reported by Kuiper, one player referred to another as a "great penis."[8] By saying this, the insulter meant to imply not that the player *has* a great—meaning particularly large or effective—penis, but that the player *is* an oversized penis and is therefore unlikely to be very good at rugby. Players who get angry at such teasing—or even worse, respond to it with hurt feelings—will soon be ostracized by the other players.

Why engage in this ritual of teasing? According to Kuiper, because it creates solidarity among the team members, albeit a coercive form of solidarity. It also ensures that team members will show no fear and will expend maximum effort during games.[9] They are fully aware, after all, that they could be called the same names in public as they are called in the privacy of the locker room, and as Kuiper puts it, with commendable understatement, "if others outside the group know that one is thought by one's male friends to be involved in bestial anal intercourse, one is unlikely to be thought well of" by the outsiders in question.[10]

IN CONCLUSION, playful teasing is one important way in which social bonds are strengthened. You don't, if you have any sense, tease strangers on the bus, since they will find your behavior insulting. Nor do you tease people you have just met. But if you know someone and want your relationship with that person to be even closer, teasing is one way to achieve your goal. Teasing implies a level of acceptance and even intimacy. Indeed, if no one ever teases you, it could well be because you don't have any close friends.

Men in particular are likely to be more comfortable with affectionate teasing than they are with outright declarations of affection. They therefore enter into the sort of joking relationships I have described. Strangers who watch "joking friends" interact with each other might mistakenly think they are bitter enemies, when in fact the insults and counterinsults being unleashed are the sign of a deep and abiding friendship.

Psychologists have documented the paradoxical nature of teasing: it can simultaneously criticize and compliment someone, and it can express affection for him by attempting to humiliate him.[11] Teasing is a form of permitted disrespect.[12] By teasing someone, we display, in a socially acceptable manner, our affection toward the target of our teasing.[13] And if we tease someone in public, we make it clear to all those who witness the tease that we have a close relationship with the target of our teasing.[14] Indeed, these witnesses might find themselves wishing that they knew the target well enough to tease him.

Think about what happens when you join a group. At first, you might find that group members, who tease each other relentlessly, treat you with respect and as a result are a bit standoffish. You realize, though, that playful teasing is a sign of social acceptance and therefore that being teased by group members is a good thing, if your goal is to become an accepted member of the group. You might therefore long to be teased by other members, and you might even go out of your way to become the target of their playful teasing. As the other group members get to know you, you might be subjected to the occasional friendly gibe. Then, if you are lucky, the day finally arrives when the group confers an affectionate nickname on you or makes you the butt of a joke. At this point, you can breathe a sigh of relief: the fact that the group abuses you means that they have embraced you as one of their own.

INSULTS OFTEN HAVE ENTERTAINMENT VALUE for the person who inflicts them, but sometimes they provide entertainment for other people as well, including their intended target. Consequently, these insults, like those involved in playful teasing, count as benign.

For examples of insults-as-entertainment, we can head to a comedy club. We will notice that some people choose to sit right in front of the stage, since doing so increases the chance that the comedian will insult them. Or we can go to a Renaissance festival, at which we might encounter an actor, dressed in period costume, who for a small fee will insult the person of our choosing in proper Elizabethan fashion. Some people, we will discover, pay this actor to insult themselves. (If these same individuals were computer-savvy, they could, for no money at all, have their computer insult them in proper Elizabethan fashion.)

When two people are well-matched in their ability to inflict insults, they might take delight in insulting each other. It is the verbal equivalent of tennis: one person hits the ball over the net, only to have the other person send it back. Such interactions, besides being entertaining to those who participate, can be entertaining to those who witness the interaction. When one person insults another, it creates a dramatic tension. Those who witness the insult will want to see how things turn out, and if the target of the insult responds with a clever repartee, they will be delighted. "I wish I could do that," they will say to themselves.

In some cultures, insults are exchanged as part of a game. In the early 1960s, for example, American blacks played a game called "the dozens." According to ethnologist Roger D. Abrahams, the game would begin when one young male insulted another's relatives. The boys who witnessed this exchange would encourage the insulted boy to respond. To defend his honor and that of his family, the reply had to be marginally clever. Thus, if the first boy had said "Your mother eats s—t," the second boy might reply "Your mother eats s—t with mustard." The first boy would then reply to the reply, and so it would go, back and forth. The game would end when a boy was unable to reply to an insult, in which case he lost. Alternatively, the game would end when the group got bored or distracted or, more rarely, when one boy hit the other.[15]

More recently, the MTV network has produced a television show called *Yo Momma* that is an updated version of the dozens game. In one part of the show, contestants exchange insults of each other's mothers. Some examples: "Yo momma's so stupid, I saw her in the kitchen peeling M&Ms, trying to make chocolate chip cookies,"[16] and "Yo momma's [bleep] is so loose that when her waters broke, Free Willy, an empty Yoo-hoo bottle, two hangers, and you fell out."[17]

Insult-swapping games are popular around the globe. In Turkey, for example, boys aged eight to fourteen exchange insults in accordance with certain rules. Most important, the reply to an insult has got to rhyme with the insult and has got to force the insulter into a female, passive role.[18] Thus, if someone calls you a bear (in Turkish, *ayi*), with the implication being that you are clumsy, big, and stupid, you might reply, *"sana girsin keman yayi,"* which means "may the bow of a violin enter your anus."[19] If you are unable to come up with a rhyming reply—or, worse still, if you are unable to come up with any reply at all—you will have lost the duel, and you will thereby, according to folklorists who have studied the game, be "reduced to the female receptive role."[20] By playing this game, Turkish boys are asserting their masculinity and jockeying for social dominance within their peer group.[21]

IN AMERICA, people who wouldn't dream of playing the dozens or even watching someone play it might nevertheless enjoy participating in what is called a *roast*. The participants in a roast insult their honored guest, who might be a friend, coworker, or relative. Meanwhile, the roasted individual sits smiling and absorbs, meekly, whatever abuse they hurl at him.

If you are a celebrity in America, being roasted by your fellow celebrities is a sign that you have arrived. The insults at celebrity roasts can be rather vicious. Consider, by way of illustration, comedienne Joan Rivers's comments at a roast of Elizabeth Taylor, given at a time when Taylor had gained considerable weight: "Liz is so fat—her favorite food is seconds; she goes through a revolving door in two trips."[22] "Liz fat? During her vacation in Florida she was ejected from a local beach for creating too much shade."[23] "It was so embarrassing— I took her to Sea World. Shamu the Whale jumped up out of the water, and Liz asked if it came with vegetables."[24] These are comments which, if uttered under normal circumstances, would likely turn Taylor into a bitter enemy of Rivers, but uttered in the course of a roast, they provoked only laughter.

Why, one wonders, would celebrities agree to be roasted? Here is a theory. We love to watch as people rise out of cultural anonymity to become famous. Part of the reason we love rising stars, I think, is that their rise nourishes our dream of someday rising out of cultural anonymity ourselves—of gaining enough fame that even strangers will admire us. But although we love to watch stars rise, we hate it when they look down on us. If we detect an element of condescension in them, we start rooting against them. We start wanting to see them fail in all they do and plunge into cultural oblivion—to rejoin, that is, the rest of us. Celebrities can avoid creating this kind of ill will in their fans and peers by submitting to celebrity roasts. It says to the world that they can still laugh at themselves and that despite their fame, they still take themselves to be "one of us."

ENTERTAINERS AREN'T the only ones who agree to be publicly roasted. In the previous chapter, I mentioned that Bill Clinton had been sarcastically cheered by the audience when he gave a speech to nominate Michael Dukakis as the presidential candidate of the Democratic Party. The event made Clinton look like a political windbag and thereby put his own political aspirations in jeopardy. Indeed, had Clinton responded to the abuse by announcing that "I should have known better than to cast my pearls before swine," he might have had a hard time winning another election.

But Clinton didn't respond to the audience's insult by returning the insult. Instead, he used the failed speech as an opportunity to engage in a bit of self-deprecating humor.

He made jokes about how bad the speech was: "It wasn't my finest hour. It wasn't even my finest hour and a half." A few nights after the failed speech, he went on *The Johnny Carson Show*. Before Clinton came on stage, Carson warned the audience not to worry, since "we've got plenty of coffee and extra cots in the lobby." Then he gave Clinton an introduction that went on and on. And after Clinton had come on stage and sat down, Carson brought an hourglass from beneath his desk and set it down. After that, Carson made jokes at Clinton's expense, and more important, Clinton made jokes at his own expense. When Carson asked Clinton if he thought he had a political future, he answered, "it depends on how I do on this show tonight." This was a joke, of course, but one that expressed a profound truth: by allowing himself to be laughed at in public, Clinton proved to the world that he wasn't a political windbag—that he was, to the contrary, "one of us" and therefore was someone we should consider voting for.[25]

Having said all this, I should add that there is a fine line between letting the world laugh at you and becoming a public laughingstock. Along these lines, consider the fate of nineteenth-century theologian and philosopher Søren Kierkegaard. Peder Møller, a former classmate of Kierkegaard, published an essay critical of both Kierkegaard's writing and Kierkegaard himself. Kierkegaard responded by publishing an article in which he attacked Møller. He pointed out, among other things, that Møller wrote for a satirical and therefore disreputable newspaper called the *Corsair*.

In the process of attacking Møller, Kierkegaard challenged the *Corsair* to mock him, in the apparent belief that such mockery could do him no harm. The newspaper accepted the challenge and started heaping abuse on Kierkegaard, who as a result became the laughingstock of Copenhagen. Everyone felt free to insult him. The experience proved to be remarkably painful: it was, Kierkegaard said, like being trampled to death by a flock of geese.[26]

LET ME END this discussion of benign insults by describing one last example. Insults, besides giving rise to disputes, can be used to settle them. Consider the "song duels" of the Eskimos of the Central Arctic. At community festivals, one man would initiate a duel by stepping forward and singing a song that contained insults and accusations of another man. The accused man would sing back his reply, which would include more insults and accusations. The insults in question, though, had to be couched in humor; the encounter had to be in a spirit of good fun, even though the underlying grievances might be quite serious. Songs would be sung back and forth until one singer was laughed down by the audience, was completely humiliated, or failed to reply.[27]

Are the insults unleashed in these song duels really benign? The person inflicting them, after all, intends to harm the other person and ruin his image in the eyes of the community. Although the insults do indeed have a malicious component, I would argue that their use was quite beneficial to the Eskimos who used them. It should be realized, in particular, that Eskimos who could not settle disputes with insulting songs might instead have resorted to violence. Indeed, in the absence of police, an Eskimo who felt sufficiently insulted might, as we shall see in the next chapter, have murdered the person who insulted him.

IT SHOULD BY NOW BE CLEAR that within the broad category of insults, there is a subgroup of what might be called *un-sults*. Whereas most insults cause a degree of pain in their targets, un-sults trigger delight. This is certainly true of playful teasing. Such teasing is often, after all, evidence of affection; indeed, we might find it distressing if, out of the blue, a friend stopped teasing us. Playful teasing is also socially useful, inasmuch as it gives people a way to deal, in a nonconfrontational manner, with the issues that inevitably arise in long-term relationships. This is part of the reason husbands and wives tease each other, as do bosses and employees. It would therefore be a mistake to assume that insults invariably represent a social evil. Indeed, if the sorts of benign insults described in this chapter were impossible, society as we know it would be difficult to maintain.

PART TWO

Insult Psychology

CHAPTER 6

A World of Hurt

MANY INSULTS, as we have seen, are benign. A person joining a group might be delighted when other group members start insulting him; such insults, after all, can be a sign of group acceptance. Other insults, though, are not welcomed by their target for the simple reason that being insulted can be an excruciatingly painful experience.

The pain in question can be physical: suppose someone insults you by slapping your face. Or it can be mental: suppose someone, rather than slapping you, calls you an idiot in public. And finally, the pain of an insult can be both physical and mental: suppose the French horn player of an orchestra is slapped by the conductor, in full view of the audience, for having played the wrong note. Notice that in this case, the mental pain the musician experiences might far exceed the physical pain. Indeed, the sting of the slap will be gone in a few seconds, but the searing emotional pain caused by the slap might last a lifetime.

Because of their pain-causing potential, insults can be enormously destructive to human relationships: a ten-word insult can, in under ten seconds, destroy a relationship that has lasted ten years. Why should this be? Why are insults so potent? In this chapter and the two that follow, I will try to answer these questions.

INSULTS CAUSE PAIN by giving rise to various negative emotions, with feelings of anger being at the top of the list. Indeed, I think it is safe to say that most of the anger people experience is triggered by the insults of others. It is possible to be mad at *something*—at, for example, the computer that just erased your data files. But usually when people are mad, they are mad not at something but at *someone*, and the reason they are mad is because the person in question said something insulting or acted in an insulting manner.

Once angered by an insult, people can respond in a number of ways. If they are clever and possess a degree of self-control, they might respond with a witty counterinsult. But if they are sufficiently angry and words fail them, they might respond by physically attacking the insulter, and the attack in question might be savage. In 2006, for example, Ronald Johannes, manager of a Burger King restaurant in the Bronx, allegedly shot and killed sixteen-year-old Shaka Walcott. Described as a quiet person, Johannes had had numerous run-ins with local teens. According to witnesses, the alleged shooting was triggered in part by Walcott's having spit in Johannes's face.[1] In another such case, Tyler Peterson, a sheriff's deputy in a tiny town in Wisconsin, went to a party to talk to a former girlfriend. She rebuffed him and, to make matters worse, the other people at the party called him a worthless pig. Petersen allegedly went to his car, got a rifle, and fired thirty shots into the crowd, killing six people.[2]

And it isn't just in advanced industrial societies that an insult can provoke homicide. In the previous chapter, I described the song duels Eskimos used to settle disputes. Sometimes, though, disputes got out of hand before a festival was held during which a song duel could be performed. In such cases, murder could ensue. Anthropologist Knud Rasmussen, in his 1931 account of Eskimo life, describes one such case. The Eskimos in question were hunting partners. One day, one of the hunters insulted the other by smearing muck on his face. The insulted Eskimo did not respond immediately to this insult, but as time passed, his anger grew. Here is his account of what happened next: "The treatment I had received tormented me so much that I could not tell anyone about it. Hatred grew up in me, and every time I met [the insulter] out caribou hunting it was as if I loathed myself; thoughts that I could not control came up in me, and so one day when we were alone together up in the mountains, I shot him."[3] He did this, I should add, knowing that he would be punished, either by the murdered man's relatives or by the white man's government.

The interesting thing about the anger caused by insults is that it often isn't a one-time thing. Rather, it gives rise to a kind of posttraumatic stress syndrome: when they least expect it, people find themselves getting angry again at insults that took place months or even decades before. I occasionally experience this phenomenon. I will, for example, be lying comfortably in bed thinking about nothing when suddenly the memory of some long-ago insult will pop into my head. Such memories, I have found, are utterly involuntary. Not only that, but once they enter my mind, they are both quite unpleasant and very difficult to extinguish. They therefore have the power to ruin a night of sleep.

WHEN SOMEONE INSULTS us in public, we are likely to experience, besides anger, a number of negative social emotions. Suppose, for example, that while washing his hands in a restroom, a man accidentally splashes water on his pants, and suppose that as he is leaving the restroom, one of his oafish friends sees him and shouts out: "Look at that! He wet himself!" It is an insult that, depending on how sensitive the man is and depending on who else hears the insult, might, besides making him mad, make him feel foolish or embarrassed; indeed, it might humiliate or, worse still, mortify him.

The words *humiliate* and *mortify* tell us something about how intense the pain caused by insults can be. *Humiliate* derives from the Latin *humus*, meaning *ground*. How does it feel to be humiliated? It feels like someone has pushed you to the ground and treated you like dirt. *Mortify*, in turn, derives from the Latin *mortificare*, meaning *to kill*. If an insult mortifies you, you will feel as if you are socially dead—as if you can no longer face the people in front of whom you were insulted. Indeed, to escape their gaze, you might wish you could crawl into a hole or hide in a closet somewhere. And in an extreme case of mortification, you might not only wish you were dead but might kill yourself in order to bring your insult-induced pain to an end.

We have considered the way sarcasm can be used in insults. The word *sarcasm* comes from the Greek *sarkazein*, meaning *to tear flesh.* To be exposed to sarcasm, then, is to feel like your flesh is being torn.

One particularly interesting negative emotion that is sometimes experienced in response to an insult is what we call *hurt feelings.* Because these feelings generally occur in conjunction with other negative emotions, it can be difficult to isolate them, but psychologists who have studied hurt feelings have observed that unlike other negative emotions, hurt feelings have a "poignant quality" which has been described, variously, as a "psychic ache," a "cutting stab," or a "painful emotional twinge."[4]

It would be hard to explain the concept of hurt feelings to someone who had never experienced them, but since nearly everyone has, such explanations are unnecessary. According to one survey of university students, 60 percent had experienced hurt feelings more often than once a month, and 20 percent had experienced hurt feelings at least once a week.[5] Researchers were unable to find a person whose feelings had never been hurt; indeed, they conclude that the inability to experience hurt feelings is likely a symptom of a serious psychological disorder.[6]

It is one thing to insult someone in a manner that makes him angry; it is quite another to insult him in a manner that hurts his feelings. Suppose, for example, I call a friend an idiot in front of a woman he is trying to impress. If you tell me that he is mad at me for doing this, I might respond that it was my goal to make him mad—that, perhaps, I was paying him back for some past insult of me. Or I might respond that even though I didn't intend to make him mad, I am not worried: he is a big boy and will get over his anger. But if you tell me that my insult has hurt his feelings, I am likely to get flustered. Hurt feelings are, after all, a serious business. I might tell you that this is the last thing I wanted to do and might ask for your advice on what, if anything, I can do to restore his feelings.

FEELINGS OF ANXIETY are another negative emotion we might experience on being insulted. Suppose, by way of illustration, that after someone insults us, we consider the things we can do in response. One option is to do nothing at all—to "take" the insult. Most people, however, will reject this option out of hand. They reject it because they fear that unless they respond to an insult—indeed, unless they respond in a forceful manner—the person who insulted them will take their nonresponse as license to insult them, and he will subsequently do so again—and again and again. And their fears regarding the insult will be heightened if it took place in front of an audience. They will then worry that members of the audience will join the insulter in insulting them.

Thus, in most of the cases in which someone is insulted, the insulted person, if questioned, will admit that the insult itself wasn't so bad, that it did him negligible harm. He will quickly add, though, that unless he nips the insulter's insulting tendencies in the bud, there is a danger that those tendencies will not only get worse but will infect other people. In other words, insulted people, when deciding how to respond to an insult, are gripped by the fear that if they let an insulter get away with one small insult today, their life will be a living hell tomorrow.

Such fears, to be sure, are not without foundation. Most of us have seen this sort of thing happen. In particular, we may have known—or may have been—a child who became, through no fault of his own, a designated target for the scorn of his peers. The other children interacted with this child only to heap invective upon him. And even worse, on gaining the status of designated target for insults, a child has a good chance of retaining it: research has shown that 30 to 45 percent of children rejected by their peers in this manner were still rejected four years later.[7] (It is also possible, as we saw in the previous chapter, for an adult to become a designated target for insults: this was the fate of Søren Kierkegaard.)

Because we fear the consequences of allowing insults to go unanswered, we tend to turn a molehill of an insult into a mountain. For a dramatic example of this, consider again the Eskimo case described above. The hunter who killed his partner justified doing so by saying that he feared for his life. More precisely, he was afraid that if he didn't respond aggressively to his partner's insults, they would intensify, and the partner would ultimately inflict on him the worst possible physical insult—namely, murder. To prevent this from happening, he killed his partner. To his way of thinking, then, it was a form of proactive self-defense.[8]

To UNDERSTAND the pain-causing potential of insults, we need to appreciate the extent to which we humans are social animals. We want, first of all, to be among other people: deprive us of human contact by putting us in solitary confinement or banishing us to a desert island, and our mental health will be in jeopardy. And once we find ourselves among other people, new social needs arise. We will, to begin with, seek to form and maintain relationships with the people around us. We will want, in particular, for some people to become our friends or lovers. We will also want to belong to groups. Indeed, according to psychologist Mark Leary and his colleagues, we are willing to expend effort to maintain connections with even "seemingly meaningless groups." This demonstrates, he says, the intensity of our need to belong.[9]

On joining a group, we will notice that group members have sorted themselves into a social hierarchy, and we will soon learn our position on that hierarchy. Some group members, we will probably discover, are above us. As a result, we will try hard to please them. We might publicly express our admiration of them—and privately experience feelings of envy toward them. We might feel slightly nervous in their presence, and we might routinely defer to their judgment and wishes. We won't enjoy being socially submissive in this manner, but unless we are exceptional individuals, we will find that we cannot help ourselves.

We are also likely to find, though, that other people in the group are below us on the group's social hierarchy. We might bask in the admiration of these social underlings and enjoy the way they do things calculated to please us. We will be careful, though, not to be openly appreciative; otherwise, they might misinterpret our social generosity as a sign of social submissiveness and might start thinking they are above us on the social hierarchy. We can't let that happen. Indeed, if they start getting uppity, we might have to put them in their place with a well-aimed insult.

IT IS BECAUSE we are social animals that insults are painful. As social animals, we seek to form relationships with others. Therefore, when someone with whom we have a personal relationship insults us, we take it as evidence that they don't value their relationship with us as highly as they once did or as highly as we might like them to,[10] and we are pained. And because we are social animals, we seek to gain and maintain as high a position as we can on the social hierarchy. Therefore, when someone insults us—even if we don't have a close personal relationship with him—we take it as evidence that he views himself as being above us on the social hierarchy, and we are again pained. If we didn't want to form and maintain close relationships with other people, and if we didn't care about our position on the social hierarchy, these insults wouldn't bother us; but we do care, so they do bother us.

Once we understand this, we are in a position to answer a number of questions about the pain-causing potential of insults.

Why are the most painful insults we experience likely to come from those with whom we have close personal relationships? The closer a relationship is, the more likely we are to value it: after all, if we didn't value a relationship, we would not have invested the effort necessary to make it close. And the more we value a relationship, the greater our sense of loss will be, and the more intense our pain will therefore be, on getting evidence, in the form of an insult, that the other party to the relationship has devalued it. Indeed, psychologists who have studied the phenomenon of hurt feelings have discovered that they are almost invariably triggered by relational devaluations.[11] Furthermore, they have discovered that how hurt someone's feelings are depends on the significance of the devaluation in question.[12]

Suppose, by way of illustration, that I am on a crowded bus, sitting next to an unused seat. Suppose that when a stranger boards the bus and asks if I mind her sitting there, I tell her that I do mind. She will take this as an insult and will probably get mad at me, but it is unlikely that her feelings will be hurt by my refusal. Suppose, however, that it is a friend who boards the bus and that I similarly reject her request to sit next to me. In this case, she might or might not get mad at me, but there is an excellent chance that her feelings will be hurt. She will take my refusal as evidence that I have devalued my relationship with her, and she might grieve the loss of this relationship. This sense of loss is presumably what makes hurt feelings hurt the way they do.

Why is it distressing to hurt someone's feelings? Above I described how, when I discover that I have hurt someone's feelings, I experience a degree of anguish that I don't experience when I insult someone in a way that merely makes him mad. This happens, I think, because to hurt someone's feelings, you must have a relationship with him that can be devalued; but it is unlikely that you would have a relationship with someone unless you valued that relationship to some extent—unless, that is, you cared about that person. Therefore, when you hurt someone's feelings, you are generally harming someone you care about. Most people won't want to do this, and if they discover that they have done it inadvertently, they are likely to feel distressed.

Why are we (as we saw in chapter 3) so sensitive to implied insults? Because when people want less of a relationship with us than we want with them, they are unlikely to come right out and say so. Similarly, when people feel that they are above us on the social hierarchy, they usually don't tell us. We find this out early in life, and as a result we develop considerable skill at "reading" other people. When we talk to them, we pay attention to their body language, to their choice of words, and to pauses in the flow of their conversation. These are subtle clues that indicate what, despite their assertions to the contrary, they really think of us.

By way of illustration, suppose that when we invite someone to go to the movies with us, they immediately respond, "Of course I'll come!" We will conclude that they value their relationship with us, or at least value the movie-going component of that relationship. Suppose, however, that instead of giving this response immediately, they wait five seconds before giving it, and suppose that during this pause, they appear to be carefully considering their options. If we have a well-developed social sense, we might conclude that they don't really want to go to the movies with us and, indeed, that they value their relationship with us less than we value our relationship with them.

Along similar lines, suppose a husband forgets his wife's birthday or their anniversary. The wife might reason that if he valued his relationship with her, he would have remembered these dates. Or suppose a husband tells his wife that he won't be home for dinner because he is going out drinking with the guys. The wife might reason that her husband has come to value his relationship with his friends more than he values his relationship with her. In either case, the wife will feel insulted by implication and might therefore experience hurt feelings.

It is important to realize, in these cases, that the wife can experience hurt feelings even if her husband in fact values his relationship with her as much as ever; what matters is whether she *feels like* he has devalued it. It is also important to realize that the wife might not blame her husband for devaluing his relationship with her; she might instead blame herself. She might, for example, think that her husband has lost interest in her because she is no longer young, because she has lately been crabby, or because she has gained weight. For this reason, notes psychologist Kristin Sommer, a relational devaluation "not only severs a potentially important relational attachment but also poses a strong threat to one's overall sense of worth."[13]

Why are people more predisposed to feel insulted in an insecure relationship than in a secure one? Because in a secure relationship, it will take a considerable body of evidence to convince one person that the other has devalued the relationship. I just described a woman who took her husband's desire to go out drinking with the guys as evidence that he had devalued his relationship with her. If she were convinced that her husband truly loves her, though, it would take more than this to make her think that his love for her has cooled. (It might, for example, take his telling her that he won't be home for dinner because he is going out drinking with his beautiful new secretary.) Likewise, in a secure marriage, if a husband forgets his wife's birthday or their anniversary, she might, rather than concluding that he loves her less, conclude that her loving husband is simply a forgetful person or that he has lately been under considerable stress.

Why aren't we pained by playful teasing? Because the insults involved in teasing, rather than being evidence that a relationship has been devalued, are evidence that a strong bond exists between the insulter and the insulted. It is for this reason that a young man might be delighted when his new girlfriend comes up with a slightly insulting pet name for him: she wouldn't do this if she didn't care for him. And it is for this reason, as we have seen, that someone who has joined a group might long for the day when group members, rather than treating him with dignified respect, start having fun at his expense. It is, after all, a sign that they have accepted him as a full-fledged member of the group. Social acceptance feels as good as social rejection feels bad.

Why does the pain caused by an insult depend on the source of the insult? If your doctor says you need to lose some weight, you are unlikely to get upset; if your lover says the same thing, you might feel both angry and hurt. Thus, whether or not a comment counts as an insult depends on who said it. If you have a close, personal relationship with someone, and if the comment implies that the other person has devalued that relationship, the comment will cause you pain. Your relationship with your lover is both close and personal; your relationship with your doctor is not. With no relationship to be devalued, you will be disinclined to "take personally" and therefore feel insulted by your doctor's lengthy and rather detailed description of your shortcomings.

Why do dogs (as I argued in chapter 2) have the power to insult us? Because we want to have relationships with them—not human relationships but relationships that are in some sense personal and that can be quite important to us. If our dog prefers someone else's company to our own, we might conclude that he values his relationship with us less than he formerly did or less than we want him to. If we love our dog, this realization will be painful.

Why is it more painful to be insulted in front of an audience than in private? Partly because of the anxiety, described above, that such insults trigger: we worry that those who witness or hear of an insult will also start insulting us. And why don't we want others to start insulting us? Because if they do, we fear that we will lose something we value—namely, our position on the social hierarchy.

Why are the silent treatment and shunning (as we saw in chapter 3) so distressing? When we experience the silent treatment from, say, a parent, we are forced to maintain a relationship with someone who, through his persistent silence, reminds us many times a day that he has devalued his relationship with us. And when we are shunned by members of a community, as sometimes happens to the Amish, we are given incontrovertible evidence that we have fallen to the bottom of that community's social hierarchy.

Why does it feel good to be praised and feel even better to be praised in public? Praise is the opposite of insults. If insults feel bad in part because they indicate that people have devalued their relationships with us, then praise feels good because it indicates that people have elevated those relationships. And if private praise feels good, public praise feels even better, inasmuch as it might lead those who witness or hear of it to accept and appreciate us. If this happens, our position on the social hierarchy might rise. In other words, praise feels good because it is evidence that our need for personal relationships and social status is being met.

Why are ambush insults, in which a person praises someone only as a setup for a subsequent insult, so painful? By initially praising us, the person gives us evidence that he thinks more highly of his relationship with us than he previously did—that he has elevated the relationship. This way, when he goes on to deliver his insult, we will measure the devaluation of the relationship not from the old level, but from a new, higher level. The perceived relational devaluation will be greater, and a greater devaluation translates into increased pain.

ALTHOUGH OUR DESIRE for personal relationships and social status explains a lot about why insults are painful, it doesn't explain everything. Suppose, for example, that a woman publishes a poem about how cruel strangers can be. Suppose that later on, she receives an anonymous letter—from, apparently, a cruel stranger—that contains a vicious parody of her poem. She will probably be angered by this insult. Her anger, though, cannot be explained in terms of a relational devaluation. She hasn't, after all, any idea who the insulter is; it is therefore unreasonable for her to draw the conclusion that the parodist has devalued his relationship with her. Nor is it reasonable for her to think that being sent this letter will cause other people to send similar letters or affect her position on the social hierarchy; this was not, after all, a public insult. The pain the letter causes her must therefore have some other source.

The obvious candidate for this other source is her self-image. The woman just described sees herself as a competent poet. The letter she was sent challenged this self-image, and it is a challenge, moreover, that went to the core of her being: if she is not who she thinks she is, then who is she? This is why the letter pained her.

We are all many things, but we pick out some of the things we are as being our defining characteristics. Thus, the woman just described might, besides being a poet, be a wife, mother, and daughter. She might also be a cook, gardener, and golfer. She has decided, though, that of all these things, being a poet is especially significant. Indeed, she might readily admit that she isn't much of a wife and that she is an incompetent golfer, but she will proudly defend her poetical abilities. It is these abilities—along, probably, with a few others—that lie at the core of her self-image.

Besides defining themselves in terms of their abilities, people define themselves in terms of their accomplishments (such as being a college graduate or having participated in the Olympics), their profession (being a doctor or a fireman), their ancestry (being a descendant of Mayflower Pilgrims or Chief Sitting Bull), their character traits (being loyal or courageous), their possessions (being a Rolex wearer or a homeowner), their political beliefs (being a dyed-in-the-wool Marxist or a libertarian), their interests (being an art lover or a sports fan), or in yet other terms. Having a self-image helps us sort out our priorities and thereby helps us determine what, in the course of a day, we ought to do. As a result, people with different self-images will have interestingly different lives.

An easy way to discover your self-image is to write down the three or so phrases that best describe you. By performing this exercise, a person might come to realize that he considers himself to be, above all else, a courageous, Rolex-wearing college graduate. And if he repeats this exercise over the years, he will probably discover that his self-image has evolved with the passage of time: in a decade, for example, *Rolex-wearer* might have been replaced by *father*. And with this change in self-image, there will typically be a corresponding change in his lifestyle.

It is understandable that people would form a self-image: if they didn't, their lives would consist of a hodge-podge of unconnected activity, and it is unlikely that they would thrive. If, however, they take themselves to be above all, say, a mother, a loyal person, and an art lover, they will know what they need to do to live in accordance with their self-image and as a result, their days will likely be spent in purposeful activity.

It is possible for us to keep our self-image to ourselves, but we rarely do. Instead, we go out of our way to project our self-image—to do things to make other people aware of who we think we are. Thus, the woman described above might have "POETESS" as her vanity license plate or a bumper sticker that says, "I'm a poet, and I know it." She might make a point of carrying around the collected poems of Emily Dickinson, not so she can read them in spare moments but as a kind of fashion accessory. She might also tell us, in casual conversation, about how she spent the first week of June at a workshop for poets: "The instructor there said I have a real gift!"

This raises a new question: why do we feel compelled to project our self-image? Why not keep it a secret? We share our self-image with others, I think, as part of a strategy to attain or maintain a certain position on the social hierarchy.

It is impossible to get other people to admit that we are admirable in every respect. We realize this and therefore implement Plan B: we set about trying to get other people to admit that we are admirable in certain respects. Thus, the woman described above may not be an admirable golfer, but this does not upset her. She thinks, however, that her poetic abilities are admirable, and she wants the rest of us to admire her accordingly.

As soon as we reveal our self-image to others, though, we open ourselves to attacks. Suppose that on learning of our self-image, someone questions whether it is an appropriate self-image—whether, that is, it corresponds to reality. If they challenge our self-image in private, their challenge can be quite painful: they might make us doubt that we are who we think we are. The attack on us, though not physical, is very real, inasmuch as it goes to the core of our self-perceived being. And if they challenge our self-image in public—by, say, creating a website that mocks us—the pain we experience is compounded: the challenge, besides making us doubt our self-image, can jeopardize our standing on the social hierarchy. Suppose we have been telling people that we should be admired for, say, being a gifted poet but that when they see our poems, they find them lacking. The people we were trying to impress, instead of looking up to us, will look down on us. Ouch!

We all recognize how painful attacks on self-image can be. As a result, we form unspoken pacts to help each other preserve our self-images.[14] Thus, in a group conversation, if someone says something, either accidentally or intentionally, that challenges a group-member's self-image, another member of the group is likely to intervene and say something that will allow the challenged person to save face. They might chide the critical individual for saying what he did. They might also provide evidence for the veracity of the self-image, even though they themselves question it.

So far in this chapter, we have considered the emotions of the person who is insulted. Let us now turn our attention to the emotions experienced by the insulter.

It is possible, to begin with, for people to enjoy insulting others. Samuel Johnson, for example, seems to have taken delight in inflicting witty invectives on other people: to insult, he tells us in his dictionary, is "to treat with insolence or contempt;...to trample upon; to triumph over."[15] If feels good, as we have seen, to gain evidence of our superior position on the social hierarchy. But it is also possible for the author of an insult to experience not so much delight as anxiety. Insulting others is, after all, a risky business. There is always the chance that the target of an insult will come back with a clever reply that makes the insulter look like a fool. And if you insult someone in front of an audience, there is the chance that the audience will side with the person you are insulting (perhaps to help him save face), in which case it is *you* who will be humiliated.

Those wishing to avoid these risks might restrict themselves to insulting only safe targets—people who can be counted on not to reply cleverly to their insult and who have few friends willing to defend them. Or they can, instead of insulting someone to his face, insult him behind his back. By doing this, they might hope to damage the insulted person's social standing without his being able to defend himself, since he doesn't know he has been insulted. Even this strategy, though, can give rise to anxieties, since as we saw in chapter 2, people who engage in backbiting leave themselves open to the possibility of insult-revelation blackmail.

We have seen that the insults implied by the silent treatment or shunning can be quite painful to those who experience them. Interestingly, these social punishments are also emotionally challenging for those who administer them. These last individuals, after all, must overcome what is, for most people, a natural human tendency to be kind to those around them. As a result, those who shun can be almost as uncomfortable as those who are shunned.[16] Likewise, those who inflict the silent treatment on relatives will find that it takes effort to remember not to start conversations with someone. They might, during the day, find that they wish to share a thought with someone and feel frustrated that they cannot share it with the only person who happens to be present. Those administering the silent treatment will also find that it takes effort to remember, when the person to whom they are not talking asks them a question, not to answer it or to answer it only in monosyllables. When shunning or the silent treatment comes to an end, those administering these punishments might therefore feel relieved.

Having said this, I should add that the negative emotions insulters experience are likely to pale in comparison to those experienced by the person they insulted. Indeed, in some cases, the impact of insults can be grotesquely asymmetrical. Researchers turned up a case, for example, in which a grown woman asserted that her life had been ruined by the relentless teasing she had received while in high school. When questioned, the man who had caused her this distress said that he could not remember ever having teased her.[17]

IN THIS CHAPTER, we have examined the pain caused by insults. The above analysis gives us, I think, important insight into the social predicament of human beings. We feel driven to form social relationships, but we do so knowing that some of our attempts at forming and maintaining these relationships will end in failure. We are willing to run the risk of social rejection, inasmuch as the cost of avoiding it—namely, life without social relationships—is unthinkable.

How much pain an insult causes depends on numerous factors. Who is insulting us? (A stranger? Our spouse? Our boss?) Why are they insulting us? (Are they trying to gain social dominance over us, or is it merely a tease?) And who witnessed the insult? (Just the insulter and ourselves? Our coworkers? The entire nation?) But there is another factor we haven't yet considered: the same insult uttered in the same circumstances might cause different people to experience different amounts of pain. A person who is acutely sensitive to insults—someone with a thin skin, as we say—might be cut to the quick by an insult, while a person with a thick skin might be unfazed by the same insult. Why? This is the question I will attempt to answer in the next chapter.

CHAPTER 7

Who Gets Hurt?

SOME PEOPLE ARE hypersensitive to insults. The mere hint of an insult—even the hint of an implied insult—is capable of causing them pain. These same individuals are also prone to experiencing hurt feelings; indeed, some of them spend their lives stewing in a cauldron of hurt feelings. When you have ongoing contact with these hypersensitive individuals, you learn to be very careful about what you say and do in their presence. You learn not even to tease them in a playful manner, since you know that they will not distinguish between playful and malicious teasing: for them, all teasing is hurtful.

At the other end of the sensitivity continuum, we find people who appear to be immune to insults. Some of these individuals are immune for the simple reason that they are too slow-witted to realize they have been insulted. They are oblivious to the insulting implications of what we say. They also fail to understand that our praise of them is sarcastic. There are also people, though, who are unfazed by our insults despite knowing full well that we are trying to insult them. The individuals in question, I should add, aren't simply pretending not to be upset; they are genuinely indifferent to our abuse. Let us, in this chapter, investigate the differences in people's sensitivity to insults.

SINCE INSULTS ARE PAINFUL in part because they are evidence of social rejection, we might infer that some people are unusually sensitive to insults because they are unusually sensitive to social rejection. And why would someone be hypersensitive to rejection? It might be because she has a problem with self-esteem.

When we hold other people in high esteem, we respect them as human beings. We regard them, because of the qualities they possess, as being worthy individuals who deserve our admiration. Along similar lines, when we hold *ourselves* in high esteem—when, that is, we have high self-esteem—we regard ourselves as being worthy individuals. Instead of feeling ashamed of ourselves, we feel proud. We feel we deserve whatever happiness comes our way. We feel, as they say, "good about ourselves." Indeed, when others tease us, we don't mind: we are wealthy enough in self-esteem that we can afford to let others have fun at our expense.

Philosopher and psychologist William James claimed that self-esteem is an "elementary endowment of human nature."[1] It is an endowment, however, like physical strength or intelligence: different people possess it to differing degrees. Thus, some people have high self-esteem, and others have low self-esteem.

A person's level of self-esteem will affect how he interacts with the world. In particular, people with high self-esteem are self-confident. They expect to succeed in the projects they undertake, and if, much to their surprise, they fail, they assume that the failure in question is simply a hurdle that must be cleared before they ultimately gain success. They are therefore willing to engage in risky undertakings and to persist in the face of failure.

Furthermore, people with high self-esteem expect people to go on liking them even if they fail in their undertakings. And most significantly for our current investigation, they expect other people to accept them socially; indeed, they might be shocked if someone rejected them. As psychologist Kristin Sommer puts it, "the higher one's self-esteem, the greater the perception that others will generally find one to be worthy of inclusion."[2] Along similar lines, psychologist Kristine Kelly concludes that "high self-esteem appears to buffer a person from the negative affect resulting from rejection."[3]

People with low self-esteem, by way of contrast, expect that others will be reluctant to accept them socially. They are also pessimistic regarding the projects they undertake, and they think that if they fail at something, it will cause others to reject them. "For them," says Sommer, "the prospect of failure is especially frightening."[4]

Thus, sensitivity to social rejection—and therefore to insults as well—is an important symptom of low self-esteem. This suggests that low self-esteem causes sensitivity to rejection, but as is true of many psychological phenomena, things are more complex than this. It is true that low self-esteem can cause people to find social rejection to be particularly painful, but being rejected socially can also cause people's level of self-esteem to plunge and might even trigger mental depression. Indeed, one study of preadolescent girls looked for predictors of depression and found one—low peer acceptance. In another study of children who had moved to a new school, researchers found that poor peer acceptance was associated with depressive symptoms one year later.[5] Of course, once a person is depressed, the pain caused by social rejection is intensified. What we end up with is a vicious causal circle. The mean-spirited insults that are the instruments of social rejection cause a decline in self-esteem, leading to heightened sensitivity to insults, which in turn causes an even greater decline in self-esteem.

DIFFERING LEVELS OF SELF-ESTEEM, besides affecting how painful social rejection is, affect how people respond to it. Consider first the response of individuals with high self-esteem. As we have seen, they expect to be accepted by others, but if they are rejected, they are likely to defend themselves as being worthy of social acceptance. In particular, they might, says Sommer, "attempt to refute the negative implications of rejection by enhancing their own and others' opinions of them."[6]

Individuals with low self-esteem, by way of contrast, are uncertain that they will be accepted socially. They are therefore reluctant to put themselves in situations in which social rejection is a possibility. They also engage in self-protection defenses. They might, for example, hold others at arm's length, socially speaking. Or they might tell themselves that certain people are not worth befriending, and this might lead them to make disparaging remarks about others.[7]

In other words, people with low self-esteem, besides being particularly pained by insults, are likely to insult others. It isn't that by making others look bad they make themselves look good; rather, they disparage others as a preemptive measure: they thereby make it easier, if the individuals in question reject them, to downplay the rejection. Furthermore, if their self-protection defenses fail them and someone rejects them socially, individuals with low self-esteem are likely to hold a grudge: they are unable or unwilling to forgive the person responsible for the rejection. By doing this, of course, they prevent that person from ever rejecting them again.[8]

By way of contrast, people with high self-esteem develop self-enhancement strategies that, says Sommer, "include focusing on one's positive traits, working hard to excel on difficult tasks, and, in response to interpersonal rejection, affirming one's desirability to others and reinforcing one's interpersonal relationships."[9] They are less likely to preemptively disparage others or hold a grudge against those who reject them.

IN THE PREVIOUS CHAPTER, we saw that part of the reason insults are painful is because they challenge our self-image. This suggests that how sensitive a person is to insults will depend in part on how secure her self-image is. Consider again the woman who was hurt when an anonymous letter-writer made fun of a poem she had written. Suppose this woman had been confident of her competence as a poet. This confidence might be the result of her having published many books of poetry to widespread critical acclaim. Alternatively, her confidence could stem from a delusional state of mind. In either case, it is unlikely that one poison-pen letter would have ruined her day. She would instead have dismissed the letter as the product of some would-be poet who was suffering from pangs of envy.

We have seen that people with low self-esteem are likely to be sensitive to insults. As it so happens, people with low self-esteem are also likely to have weak or ambiguous self-concepts; they have, according to psychologist Jennifer Campbell, "more poorly articulated notions of who or what they are" than do people with high self-esteem.[10] And because they are unsure of who they are, they are "more dependent on, susceptible to, and influenced by external self-relevant stimuli."[11] They are, in other words, sensitive to what other people say about them.

This raises another causal question: does low self-esteem cause a fragile self-image (as well as causing sensitivity to insults), or does a fragile self-image cause low self-esteem? I would like to suggest that although low self-esteem might be *a* cause of a fragile self-image, it cannot be *the only* cause. It is possible, after all, for a person to have a fragile self-image despite having high self-esteem. We call such people *narcissists*, and as a group they happen to be particularly sensitive to insults. This suggests that a fragile self-image can, all by itself, cause sensitivity to insults.

People with high self-esteem, then, can be divided into two groups: those with a secure self-image and those with a fragile self-image. People in both groups, thanks to their high self-esteem, will be confident and will be willing to undertake ventures that might result in failure. Those with a secure self-image will tend to undertake these ventures quietly and will not expect to be praised for undertaking them. They might also be reluctant to talk about past accomplishments.

As an example of individuals with both high self-esteem and a secure self-image, I would nominate the ancient Stoic philosophers. The Stoics, when insulted, were unlikely to do anything in response. They were also unlikely to go around insulting others and just as unlikely to praise themselves. The simplest way to explain their behavior is to conclude that practicing their philosophy somehow conferred on them both high self-esteem and a secure self-image. I will have much more to say about the Stoics and their advice regarding insults in chapters 9 and 11.

By way of contrast, those with high self-esteem but a fragile self-image—in other words, narcissists—will delight in boasting about past successes and in predicting further future success. They will openly invite our praise. And if a risky venture fails, they will be anxious to blame someone else for the failure.

A narcissist is convinced of his own importance—indeed, his own superiority. From his point of view, he is brilliant, gifted, and successful in a way that those around him aren't. Because he feels this way, he sees nothing wrong with manipulating and exploiting others to accomplish his goals. In fact, in his scheme of things, the primary role for other people—their raison d'être, as it were—is to help him get whatever it is that he wants, and to acknowledge and admire his superiority.

A narcissist will also tend to be an insulting individual: by making disparaging remarks about those around him and their achievements, he can make himself and his own achievements look that much better. Someone with high self-esteem and a secure self-image, by way of contrast, will be less likely to feel threatened by those around him and their successes. He will therefore be less likely to insult them.

Suppose we insult someone who has a fragile self-image—insult her in a way that challenges that image. She will, as we have seen, be stung by our insult. Because her self-image is fragile, she will look to the world around her for affirmation that she is who she thinks she might be, and if we challenge her self-image, it will be a painful blow to her ego. If the person we insult has a fragile self-image combined with low self-esteem, she might slink off in silence. But if the person we insult has both a fragile self-image and high self-esteem—if, that is, she is a narcissist—she might lash out at us.[12]

SUPPOSE IT WAS our goal to create a world in which the pain caused by insults was minimized. To accomplish this goal, we might take steps to prevent people from insulting others. In America and elsewhere, such steps have been taken, in the form of the political correctness (PC) movement and the enactment of hate-speech laws, about which I will say more in chapter 10. We might also want to take steps, though, to make people less sensitive to the insults we fail to prevent. And how might we accomplish this? Inasmuch as low self-esteem makes people sensitive to insults, the obvious way to desensitize people is by initiating a campaign to boost their self-esteem.

In the late 1980s, America began such a campaign. The primary goal of this campaign, to be sure, was not to make people less sensitive to insults; the goal was instead to deal with a number of social evils, including poor performance in the classroom, teen pregnancy, drug abuse, violence, and crime. Politicians, following the lead of psychologists and sociologists, argued that the best way to eradicate these evils was to eradicate the low self-esteem they thought caused them. And so began a quest to improve people's self-esteem. Before long, this quest had, according to social psychologist Roy F. Baumeister and his colleagues, become "a national preoccupation."[13]

How does one go about enhancing self-esteem? Well, if people with low self-esteem think they are not praiseworthy, the obvious way to raise their level of self-esteem is to convince them that they are praiseworthy, and what better way to do this than to praise them—to tell them repeatedly what wonderful people they are? Furthermore, it makes sense, if our goal is to boost people's self-esteem, to work with them while they are young. Children will presumably be more psychologically malleable than adults. Not only that, but if we boost people's self-esteem while they are children, they can enjoy the benefits of high self-esteem for their entire life.

It was with this reasoning in mind that in schools across America, teachers started devoting significant time and energy to telling students what wonderful human beings they were. Not only that, but they were careful to prevent students from receiving negative feedback that might damage their self-esteem. Students who learned nothing in class weren't given esteem-deflating Fs and weren't held back for a year; they were instead given passing grades and promoted to the next grade level. Students whose classroom performance was adequate weren't given Cs; they were instead rewarded with Bs or quite possibly with As. (Between 1968 and 2004, the percentage of students receiving As in high school went from 17.6 percent to 47.5 percent.)[14] And even A students weren't given what for them might be an esteem-deflating 4.0 grade average;

educators tampered with the grading scale so these students could have a grade-point average that was above the 4.0 that had formerly indicated perfection.

The self-esteem movement also affected the scoring of standardized tests. In 1994, the College Board adjusted Scholastic Aptitude Test (SAT) scores so that an effort on the English portion of the test that would have earned his parents a score of 424 earned a student a 500 (out of 800 points possible). It also became possible to achieve a "perfect" score of 1600 on the combined math and English portions of the exam despite making mistakes, and as a result, the number of students with perfect scores soared from 32 in the year before the adjustment to 545 in the year after.[15]

Even under this system of almost exclusively positive feedback, it was possible for students to do things that, to everyone involved, clearly constituted failure. In such cases, educators encouraged students to place the blame for the failure where it belonged—on someone or something other than the student. If a student got a terrible score on a standardized test, for example, it wasn't the student's fault; the test was to blame. Or maybe society was to blame, for having constructed and administered such tests.

On graduation day, educators continued their efforts to boost self-esteem. In the old days, high schools typically had one valedictorian, but educators worried that for students not to be named valedictorian would deflate the self-esteem they had worked so hard to inflate. It therefore became commonplace for high schools to name multiple valedictorians, and a high school might end up with, say, forty-one of them.[16]

And efforts to boost self-esteem weren't limited to schools. In some youth baseball and basketball leagues, for example, teams stopped keeping score; this way, no one would have to experience the agony of defeat. At track meets and science fairs, winners weren't awarded special ribbons; instead, everyone was awarded a participation ribbon. This way, everyone was a winner, meaning that everyone could enjoy the esteem-boosting effects of having won. Or at least this was the theory.

THE SELF-ESTEEM MOVEMENT was a noble experiment: those who undertook it had the best of intentions. And in one respect, the experiment was a success: it produced a generation of people who, by all accounts, thought very highly of themselves. Between the early 1950s and the late 1980s, the number of teenagers who agreed with the statement "I am an important person" increased from 12 percent to 80 percent. They also scored much higher on psychological tests of narcissistic behavior than teens of earlier generations had. In particular, they were inclined to agree with statements like these: "If I ruled the world it would be a better place" and "I am a special person."[17]

And did all this boosting of self-esteem eradicate the social evils that the movement's advocates hoped it would? Apparently not. Teenagers became more likely than ever to engage in sex, use alcohol or drugs, behave in an aggressive manner, or commit violent acts. Not only that, but research subsequently undertaken by Baumeister and his colleagues suggests that low self-esteem does not, in fact, contribute to these social maladies, meaning that boosting self-esteem could not have cured them.[18]

Baumeister's research also indicates that although steps taken to raise a student's self-esteem might inflate her grade-point average, they will not necessarily improve her academic performance; indeed, they might even impair it. It is easy to see why. Negative feedback about a student's classroom performance is painful, but it can motivate her to study harder. In the absence of such feedback, a student can take it easy. She knows, after all, that despite not opening her books, she will get good grades, will be promoted to the next grade level, will ultimately graduate, and—who knows?—might even be class valedictorian, along with a few dozen of her peers. Various statistics indicate that many students aren't learning much of anything in high school. Thanks to their heightened self-esteem, though, these same students feel good about their ignorance.

And what about sensitivity to insults? Did the self-esteem movement, as a kind of side benefit, at least create a generation of people who, when insulted, would be unfazed? Quite the contrary. The problem is that while the movement was inflating people's self-esteem, it was doing nothing to help them form a secure self-image; indeed, it was, if anything, making it harder for them to form such an image. If people get meaningful feedback about their strengths and weaknesses while growing up, they can develop a sense of what they are and aren't good at, and they can use this information to construct an appropriate self-image. Meaningful feedback might, for example, allow them to deduce that they have talent as a basketball player or as a math student, and they can include this talent among their defining characteristics.

In many cases, though, students were deprived of such feedback, for fear that it would deflate their self-esteem. They were instead praised for all they did. As a result, they concluded that they were good at everything, as was everyone else—meaning that they were, comparatively speaking, good at nothing. It is hard to form a robust self-image under these circumstances.

By inflating people's self-esteem while simultaneously hindering their ability to form a self-image, the self-esteem movement inadvertently created a generation notable for its narcissism—and narcissists, as we have seen, are quite sensitive to insults. They are also likely to be insulting individuals. On television shows such as the MTV network's *Real World*, we are treated to the spectacle of a group of these manufactured narcissists trying to live together under one roof. The cast members of this show seem remarkably susceptible to hurt feelings. They are also remarkable for the bluntness with which they insult each other. It does not appear to be a happy environment. The same can be said of subsequent reality shows, including *Jersey Shore* and the *Real Housewives* series, in which people are thrown together while cameras watch the social conflict that ensues.

In other reality shows, people compete against each other in contrived contests. Often in these shows, the performance of each contestant is judged, both cruelly and in public. Judges routinely go out of their way to intensify the anxiety a contestant is experiencing by pausing for several seconds before rendering their verdict. On encountering these shows, I was at first puzzled that anyone would want to witness these spectacles of human suffering. Then it dawned on me that these shows are vehicles for the escapist fantasies of a generation raised in a nonjudgmental environment. Someone who has never boxed might, as he watches a boxing match, imagine himself in the ring, slugging it out with a worthy opponent and ultimately triumphing. Likewise, someone who has never been judged might fantasize about someday being subjected to and successfully withstanding withering criticism. "What must it be like," they wonder, "to have someone tell you what they really think about your abilities?"

Is THERE A WAY to reduce people's sensitivity to insults without simultaneously turning them into narcissists? I think there is. Rather than trying to inflate schoolchildren's self-esteem "artificially" by heaping praise on them and withholding criticism, we should create an environment in which their self-esteem will be enhanced "naturally." We should, in particular, present them with challenges that, with effort, they can fulfill. As they fulfill these challenges, they will become increasingly self-confident, and thanks to their achievements, they will have a growing sense that they are worthwhile individuals. And at the same time as this is happening, they will gain insight into what they are good at and what they are not good at, what they like doing and what they dislike doing, and this will help them form a self-image. If all goes well, they will end up with both high self-esteem and a secure self-image. As a result, they will simultaneously be less sensitive to insults and less likely to be insulting than are narcissists or people with low self-esteem.

As part of their training, children should also be encouraged to take responsibility for their mistakes: this way, besides gaining self-esteem, they can gain what is probably even more important—namely, self-respect. It would also be a good idea to surround them with role models—adults who, because they have high self-esteem and a secure self-image, aren't particularly sensitive to insults and aren't likely to insult others. The program I have described is, of course, almost the polar opposite of the program undertaken by the proponents of the self-esteem movement.

This and the previous chapter make it clear how hurtful insults can be. And yet knowing this, we find it difficult to resist the temptation to insult the people around us. Why do we behave this way? It is to this question that we will now turn our attention.

CHAPTER 8

Why We Insult

INSULTS ARE PAINFUL, as we have seen, because we have certain social needs. We seek to be among other people, and once among them, we seek to form relationships with them and to improve our position on the social hierarchy. They are also painful because we have a need to project our self-image and to have other people not only accept this image, but support it. If we didn't have these needs, being insulted wouldn't feel bad. Furthermore, although different people experience different amounts of pain on being insulted, almost everyone will experience some pain. Indeed, we would search long and hard to find a person who is never pained by insults—or who himself never feels the need to insult others.

These observations raise a question we have not yet considered: why do we have the social needs we do? According to evolutionary psychologists, our social needs—and, more generally, our psychological propensities—are the result of nature rather than nurture. More precisely, they are a consequence of our evolutionary past. The views of evolutionary psychologists are of interest in this, a book about insults, for the simple reason that they allow us to gain a deeper understanding of why it is painful when others insult us and why we go out of our way to cause others pain by insulting them.

We humans find some things to be pleasant and other things to be unpleasant. We find it pleasant, for example, to eat sweet, fattening foods or to have sex, and we find it unpleasant to be thirsty, swallow bitter substances, or get burned. Notice that we don't choose for these things to be pleasant or unpleasant. It is true that we can, if we are strong-willed, voluntarily do things that are unpleasant, such as put our finger in a candle flame. We can also refuse to do things that are pleasant: we might, for example, forgo opportunities to have sex. But this doesn't alter the basic biological fact that getting burned is painful and having sex is pleasurable. Whether or not an activity is pleasant is determined, after all, by our wiring, and we do not have it in our power—not yet, at any rate—to alter this wiring.

Why are we wired to be able to experience pleasure and pain? Why aren't we wired to be immune to pain while retaining our ability to experience pleasure? And given that we possess the ability to experience both pleasure and pain, why do we find a particular activity to be pleasant rather than painful? Why, for example, do we find it pleasant to have sex but unpleasant to get burned? Why not the other way around? I have given the long answer to these questions elsewhere.[1] For our present purposes—namely, to explain why we have the social needs we do—the short answer will suffice.

We have the ability to experience pleasure and pain because our evolutionary ancestors who had this ability were more likely to survive and reproduce than those who didn't. Creatures with this ability could, after all, be rewarded (with pleasurable feelings) for engaging in certain activities and punished (with unpleasant feelings) for engaging in others. More precisely, they could be rewarded for doing things (such as having sex) that would increase their chances of surviving and reproducing, and be punished for doing things (such as burning themselves) that would lessen their chances.

This makes it sound as if a designer was responsible for our wiring, but evolutionary psychologists would reject this notion. Evolution, they would remind us, has no designer and no goal. To the contrary, species evolve because some of their members, thanks to the genetic luck-of-the-draw, have a makeup that increases their chances of surviving and reproducing. As a result, they (probably) have more descendants than genetically less fortunate members of their species. And because they spread their genes more effectively, they have a disproportionate influence on the genetic makeup of future members of their species.

Evolutionary psychologists would go on to remind us that if our evolutionary ancestors had found themselves in a different environment, we would be wired differently and as a result would find different things to be pleasant and unpleasant. Suppose that getting burned, rather than being detrimental to our evolutionary ancestors, had somehow increased their chances of surviving and reproducing. Under these circumstances, those individuals who were wired so that it felt good to get burned would have been more effective at spreading their genes than those who were wired so that it felt bad. And as a result we, their descendants, would also be wired so that it felt good to get burned.

Evolutionary psychologists would also remind us that the evolutionary process is imperfect. For one thing, although the wiring we inherited from our ancestors might have allowed them to flourish on the savannahs of Africa, it isn't optimal for the rather different environment in which we today find ourselves. Our ancestors who had a penchant for consuming sweet, fattening foods, for example, were less likely to starve than those who didn't. The problem is that we who have inherited that penchant live in an environment in which sweet, fattening foods are abundant. In this environment, being wired so that it is pleasant to consume, say, ice cream, increases our chance of getting heart disease and other illnesses, and thereby arguably lessens our chance of surviving.

EVOLUTIONARY PSYCHOLOGISTS Mark Leary and Erika Koch offer the following description of the social predicament of our ancestors: "In many ways, the African savannah was a relatively hospitable environment for early human beings (and their pre-human ancestors). . . . Early human beings lived as nomadic hunter-gatherers, moving about seeking edible plants and animals. The primary dangers were predators, foreign bands of potentially hostile people, and starvation, particularly when one was too young, old, ill, or injured to find food on one's own." They add that "solitary individuals could not survive for long in such an environment."[2] As a result, those of our ancestors who sought the company of other people—who found it pleasant to be part of a band and unpleasant to be alone—were far more likely to survive and reproduce than those who shunned people—who found it unpleasant to be part of a band and pleasant to be alone in the wilderness.

And once they were part of a band, our evolutionary ancestors who found it pleasant to form social relationships with other members of the band and to rise up within the band's social hierarchy were more likely to survive and reproduce than those who found these things to be unpleasant. After all, those who had friends and social status probably had better access to the band's resources, especially its supplies of food. And if an ancestor was a male, his reproductive ability was presumably a function of his social status: socially dominant males were more likely to find reproductive partners—and thereby become our evolutionary ancestors—than those at the bottom of the social hierarchy.

Having said this, I should add that although an abiding concern with their position on the social hierarchy helped our evolutionary ancestors survive and reproduce, this is no longer the case. If a modern human's position on the social hierarchy falls, he will still probably have food to eat and a roof over his head. And as far as reproduction is concerned, we need to keep in mind that those at the bottom of the social hierarchy are no longer prevented from reproducing; in fact, in many cases, they are remarkably prolific.

We are now in a position to offer a fairly complete answer to the question we raised two chapters back: why are insults painful? They are painful, as we have seen, because we have certain social needs. And why do we have these needs? Because our evolutionary ancestors who were wired to have them—wired, that is, so that it felt good to be among other people and once among them, felt good to form relationships with other individuals and to attain a certain position on the social hierarchy—were more likely to survive and reproduce than those who weren't wired in this manner. We modern humans have inherited the genes of these reproductively successful individuals, and consequently we are wired, as were they, to have social needs.

It is therefore an evolutionary accident that we have the social needs we do. If the environment of our evolutionary ancestors had been different, our social needs might also have been different. Change their environment dramatically, and we might have ended up solitary creatures like orangutans, or we might have become even more gregarious than we are.

WE HUMANS ARE WIRED with a number of biological systems. One of these systems monitors our hydration level. It operates continuously and unobtrusively; indeed, it is only when it has something to tell us—namely, that we are dehydrated—that its existence becomes apparent: it will cause us to feel thirsty.

Mark Leary has theorized the existence of another biological system that, rather than monitoring our hydration status, monitors our social status. Should our social status fall, this system will alert us by making us feel bad. Here is how Leary describes this system:

> Successfully maintaining one's connections to other people requires a system for monitoring others' reactions, specifically the degree to which other people are likely to reject or exclude the individual. Such a system must monitor one's inclusionary status more or less continuously for cues that connote disapproval, rejection, or exclusion (i.e., it must be capable of functioning preconsciously), it must alert the individual to changes in his or her inclusionary status (particularly decrements in social acceptance), and it must motivate behavior to restore his or her status when threatened.[3]

At the heart of this biological system is the "device" that Leary calls a *sociometer*.

Our sociometer is always on, running in the background. Suppose, for example, we are at a party, having a conversation with someone. Without our even realizing it, our sociometer is monitoring our social environment. Thus, when someone across the room mentions our name, our sociometer will direct our attention to that conversation. What is she saying about us? Are we being praised? Insulted? If it turns out that she is saying something negative, our sociometer, says Leary, will cause us to experience unpleasant emotions: we might, for example, experience anger. These emotions will in turn motivate us to do something to defend our social status.[4] If it turns out, though, that she is saying something nice about us, we might experience a rather different emotion, the glow of social acceptance.

Our sociometer is quite sensitive. Besides being able to detect blatant signs of a change in our inclusionary status, such as someone screaming "I hate you," it can detect subtle signs, such as pauses in a conversation or a lack of eye contact during a conversation. Indeed, our sociometer can be too sensitive: according to Leary, "people with unstable self-esteem essentially have an unstable sociometer that overresponds to cues that connote acceptance and rejection. For such people, minor changes in inclusion or exclusion result in large changes in the sociometer (and self-esteem)."[5] This would explain, of course, why people with low self-esteem find insults to be particularly painful.

Although our sociometer detects both signs of social rejection and signs of social acceptance, it is, says Leary, more sensitive to rejection than to acceptance: "Not only does a slightly negative reaction have a much greater impact on most people than even a strongly positive one, but a single negative reaction can counteract and undo a plethora of accolades."[6] Furthermore, our sociometer is self-adjusting: it is "sensitive to the idiosyncratic standards of particular people. What may not jeopardize one's image in one person's eyes may lead to rejection by another."[7] Thus, the sociometer of a teenager may take in stride an insult unleashed by a parent but set off major alarms on detecting a classmate's sarcasm.

THE THEORY THAT WE COME equipped with sociometers explains a lot—but not everything. After all, these social-rejection-detecting devices would be an utter waste unless there were a significant amount of social rejection for them to detect, much as ears would be a waste if there were never any sounds to hear. As it so happens, though, we live in a world awash with social rejection, much of it expressed with insults. Why is this? Why do we go around insulting each other?

Thanks to our evolutionary past, we regard ourselves as participants in an ongoing battle for position on the social hierarchy. Our opponents in this battle are other people, and we view the battle in question as a zero-sum game: for someone to rise on the social hierarchy, someone else must fall. In order to avoid losing ground in this battle, we behave in a defensive manner: we respond vigorously to those who insult us. And in order to gain ground, we engage in programs of social self-promotion.

Some of these programs are positive: we say nice things about ourselves so those around us will know how wonderful we are. Along these lines, we might take steps to project our self-image: besides thinking of ourselves as a poet, we might take steps to make others aware of our poetical ability so that they can admire us for it. We might also provide our friends with evidence of our popularity: a young woman, for example, might tell her friends about the parties she has been invited to or about all the men who have recently asked her out. And since, in our culture, material well-being and social prominence are connected, we might provide others with evidence of our affluence: we might, for example, wear an expensive watch or even tell them how much it cost.

It is instructive to examine the conversations we have with other people. What we will discover is that many of these conversations contain a significant element of self-promotion. Sometimes we boast outright about the wonderful things we have done. More often, though, we come up with ways to let other people know how wonderful we are without seeming boastful about it. Thus, rather than telling her friends about all the men who have recently asked her out, the young woman mentioned above might tell them that guys are driving her crazy, in the hope that they will ask for detailed information about how, exactly, they are driving her crazy. She can then report that Tom asked her out, then Dick, then Harry, and so on. In doing this, she isn't boasting; she is merely answering the question they asked.

In the last decade, many young adults have resorted to tattoos as part of their personal program of self-promotion. By getting, for example, a tattoo that says *loyalty*, they can make the world aware of a character trait that might not otherwise be obvious. And if they don't want to be quite this blatant in their self-promotion, they might ask the tattoo artist to write the self-descriptive word in a foreign language. Then, when people ask them what the tattoo means, they can humbly respond that it is, say, Japanese for *courage*.

Another recent trend is the use of the Internet for self-promotion. People create web pages to tell the world who they are, what they stand for, and what they have accomplished. They might round out this promotional effort by sending out, many times a day, messages telling what they are doing, including reports on what they are buying, what they are wearing, or where they are eating. Those who do this, I should add, are unlikely to characterize their online activities as a form of self-promotion. To their way of thinking, they are just keeping in touch with friends.

Other programs of self-promotion are negative: rather than saying nice things about ourselves, we disparage the people around us. Suppose, then, that Alice proudly tells Betty about her latest consumer purchase, a Coach brand handbag. She adds that it was a real steal—that she paid "only" $300 for it. Why is Alice telling Betty this? In part, she is simply sharing information, but there is probably also an element of self-promotion in this revelation, inasmuch as owning such a purse can, in certain circles, advance her social standing. Alice might deny having such a motive, but if so, it could well be because she does not fully comprehend the motives that lie behind her consumer purchases.

Betty, however, might react to the announcement not by admiring Alice but by envying her. Indeed, she might feel threatened by Alice's purchase: she might worry that by making it, Alice will surpass her on the social hierarchy. Consequently, Betty will find herself tempted to denigrate the purchase and thereby put Alice in her proper place on the social hierarchy—namely, somewhere below Betty. With these thoughts in mind, Betty might undertake a defensive strategy.

She could openly disparage Alice's purchase, but this could jeopardize their relationship. Better, then, to resort to subtle putdowns. Along these lines, she might tell Alice that she had considered buying that handbag but decided against it—the implication being that she didn't find it worth buying. Or she might tell Alice that if *she* were going to splurge on a handbag, she would never settle for a Coach; she would instead acquire a (rather more expensive) Louis Vuitton. Betty might also be tempted to belittle Alice's purchase to mutual friends.

MARK LEARY, AS WE HAVE SEEN, thinks our sociometer is the source of the angry feelings we experience when we have been insulted: by causing us to experience them, the sociometer motivates us to respond. This is why, when someone insults us, we feel driven to retaliate with an insult.

I would like to extend Leary's sociometer theory by suggesting that another important emotion our sociometer causes us to experience is feelings of envy in response to an indication that someone is or soon will be above us on the social hierarchy. Thus, our sociometer might trigger feelings of envy in us when a classmate is elected prom queen, a friend buys an expensive handbag, a colleague wins an award, or a teammate wins the praise of the coach. In any of these cases, our feelings of envy might cause us to unleash a *first-strike* insult against the object of our envy.

I suspect that if we analyzed the malicious first-strike insults we inflict, we would discover that feelings of envy lurk behind most of them. Envy is a fascinating emotion. It is ubiquitous, but we wouldn't know this from talking to people: although most people will readily admit that they experience anger, few will admit that they experience pangs of envy, and fewer still will admit that these pangs cause them to insult others. Envy is also an emotion that, like anger, can motivate people to do things that, as rational agents, they have no business doing. Indeed, I would argue that unless we understand envy, there is a broad range of human behavior that will baffle us.

THE THEORY THAT we are wired by evolution to care very deeply about our social status explains why virtually everyone periodically unleashes insults. It explains why, although cultures may differ in what counts as an insult, the concept of an insult is shared by all cultures. And it explains why people have apparently been insulting each other since the dawn of time.

It is important to realize that even though we have been evolutionarily programmed to do something, it is possible for us to override this programming. When lunchtime rolls around, for example, we will experience hunger pangs: they are evolution's way of getting us to eat. But if we are on a diet and have willpower, we will ignore these pangs. It is also important to realize that we did not evolve so that our chances of having a good and meaningful life would be maximized. Indeed, the evolutionary process is utterly indifferent to the quality of our life. All that matters, as far as evolution is concerned, is that creatures be likely to survive and reproduce, perhaps in misery.

Therefore, if our goal is to have a good and meaningful life, we will periodically take steps to override our evolutionary programming. We will restrain ourselves from doing things that would be pleasurable, such as having a bowl of ice cream when we are on a diet; we will also force ourselves to do things that are unpleasant, such as swallowing a bitter-tasting medicine. A person who is unwilling or unable to override extensive portions of his evolutionary programming will be unlikely to live the life of his own choosing. He will instead become a slave to pleasure, assiduously seeking to do whatever feels good and avoid doing whatever feels bad.

Among the evolutionary programming we will want to override, if we wish to have a good life, is the programming that makes us want to insult others and that makes us get angry in response to their insults of us. In part three, we will investigate how this can be done.

PART THREE

Dealing with Insults

CHAPTER 9

Personal Responses to Insults

SO FAR IN THIS BOOK, we have examined the many forms insults can take. We have also investigated why we insult others and why we find it so painful to be insulted by them. Let us now inquire how best to deal with insults. How, that is, can we minimize the harm they cause us?

In our examination of the ways in which we might deal with insults, it will be useful to distinguish between *personal* and *societal* responses. Thus, suppose a coworker calls me a white-trash honky. There are a number of ways in which I personally might respond to this insult: I might hurl back a racial epithet, I might punch him, I might cry, or I might do nothing at all. It is also possible, though, for the society of which I am part—and here, I am using the word *society* in a broad sense—to respond to this insult: my employer might chastise the insulter for using a racial epithet at the workplace, or my government might punish him for engaging in hate speech. In this chapter I will examine personal responses to insults and in the next chapter will examine societal responses.

WHAT IS THE BEST WAY for us, as individuals, to deal with insults? We should, to begin with, develop a strategy for preventing others from insulting us. One way to accomplish this is to avoid other people, but this will be hard for most of us to do: people, as we have seen, need people. A less radical insult-prevention strategy is to avoid not people in general but insulting individuals, such as the woman who, every time we encounter her, explains in detail why we will never amount to anything or the man whose idea of conversation is to remind us of the insulting things he has said or done to us in the past.

There is much to be said for this strategy, but for most people in most circumstances, it is not practicable to avoid all contact with insulting individuals. Some of these individuals, after all, will be relatives who will be encountered if we wish to attend family gatherings; others will be coworkers with whom we must deal if we wish to keep our job. This is why besides developing an insult prevention strategy, we need to develop a strategy to minimize the harm done to us by those insults we cannot prevent.

Suppose, then, that someone walks up and says something insulting. What should we do in response? One thing we can do is capitulate to the insult: we can allow ourselves to feel the pain the insulter intended to inflict. We might even burst into heartfelt tears. This might not seem like a sensible thing to do if our goal is to minimize the harm the insulter does us, but under some circumstances, capitulation can be a singularly effective weapon. It will make the insulter look cruel for having said whatever he said. Indeed, if the person insults us before an audience and if we subsequently burst into tears, it is possible that the audience will rise to defend us: "You big bully!" they will tell the insulter. "Shame on you for making this poor soul cry!" The insulter might think twice before insulting us again.

Most people, though, will be reluctant to capitulate to insults. They will instead make it clear to the insulter that they reject his criticisms. They might, in particular, attempt to refute those criticisms. Thus, if someone calls them fat, they might respond by telling him their recent body mass index (BMI) number. This will, however, be an emotionally unsatisfying way to respond to the insult. Furthermore, it is unlikely to deter the insulter from insulting them again. Indeed, in response to this refutation, he might simply call them an idiot. What will they do then, inform him of their IQ?

Another quite popular way to reject an insult is to retaliate with a counterinsult. This response seems utterly appropriate. By insulting the person who insulted us, we are following the Old Testament injunction to take an eye for an eye: we are attempting to make the insulter feel the pain he made us feel. Furthermore, if our counterinsult causes the insulter to experience enough pain, the insulter will think twice about insulting us again. Thus, by responding vigorously to an insult, we can, most people would maintain, prevent future insults. Responding to an insult with a counterinsult is also likely to be emotionally satisfying.

RETALIATORY INSULTS can be ranked on a cleverness scale. At the bottom of this scale, we find echoed insults: when someone calls you lazy, you respond by saying, "No, it is *you* who are lazy!" We also find all-purpose insults, such as flipping someone the bird—showing him, that is, your extended middle finger. These insults are easy to deliver and can be used in response to any insult someone might direct your way.

One step up from these mindless insults we find retaliatory insults that display a small degree of cleverness. If someone calls you fat, for example, you might reply, "At least when I swim in the pool, people don't mistake me for a manatee, the way they do with you." How much cleverness this insult reveals depends, of course, on whether you made it up on the spot or are merely repeating an insult you heard elsewhere.

Some people go out of their way to acquire a stockpile of insults to use in retaliation when they are insulted. The poet A. E. Housman, for example, is said to have written down in a notebook witty insults that might come in handy in the future.[1] These individuals are like people who train in the martial arts so that if someone attacks them in a dark alley, they will be able to defend themselves. And in the same way as there are people who make a living teaching martial arts, there are people who make a living—or part of one—teaching people retaliatory insults. In the introduction to his 2,000 *Insults for All Occasions*, Louis A. Safian explains that he compiles insults so people will have snappy comebacks to use when they have been insulted.[2]

Some people may be able to develop a repertoire of retaliatory insults by studying insult books, but I am not one of them. For one thing, I have a terrible memory for the sort of insults one finds in these books. (I also have a terrible memory for jokes.) And even if I could memorize a range of retaliatory insults, I am not fast enough on my feet to react to an insult with the appropriate counterinsult. Insults, when they come, tend to come out of the blue, when you least expect them: they are the verbal equivalent of sucker punches. Give me enough time, and I can think of what I should have said in response to an insult, but by then, the response is useless. I don't think I am alone in this respect.

One time when memorizing an insult might be particularly effective is if you knew you were going to encounter a predictable insulter—someone who, whenever he met you, insulted you in the same way. ("Hi, baldy!") You could be ready for him with an appropriate retaliatory insult. Better still, you could write your insult on an index card. When he came up to insult you, you could pull out the card and read him the counterinsult. You could then explain your action: "I knew you were going to insult me the way you did. For some reason, you feel compelled to insult me in this manner every time we meet. I don't know why you do it, but you do."

In a perfect world, this performance would make the insulter feel ridiculous and cure him of his predictably insulting ways. Then again, this is a lot of effort to invest in dealing with someone who is probably best ignored. Furthermore, someone who inflicts the same insult every time he meets you is probably not particularly bright. He might not, therefore, realize just how ridiculous he looks. Indeed, the next time you meet him, he might again greet you with the same old insult, and he might be a bit disappointed if you do not respond by pulling out your index card.

Now LET US TURN our attention to the retaliatory insults that occupy the upper end of the cleverness scale. We have seen that it is possible to exploit the ambiguity of words in order to insult someone. It is also possible to exploit ambiguity in a counterinsult. Suppose, for example, that someone calls us a thumb-sucking mama's boy. We might respond by saying, "That is the most intelligent thing I've ever heard you say." The insulter might initially be delighted to hear this: it sounds, after all, as if we are agreeing with him. But then he might realize that there is a second interpretation of our remark: if *this* is the most intelligent thing the insulter has said, then most of the things he says must be quite foolish indeed. Or, if someone insults us by implying that we aren't very bright, we might respond that we wouldn't for a moment suggest that our intelligence *equals* his (inasmuch as we are confident that our intelligence, rather than equaling his, *exceeds* it).

When we respond to insults with slyly ambiguous counterinsults, there is a danger that the person who insulted us is too slow-witted to realize that we have insulted him in return. Even this outcome, though, can be satisfying, inasmuch as it demonstrates, both to ourselves and to any (more quickwitted) observer of the exchange, that the person who insulted us is indeed a clod.

For even wittier comebacks to insults, we can turn to Winston Churchill, who was a master of the art of repartee. George Bernard Shaw once sent Churchill two tickets for the opening night performance of one of his plays, with a note that read, "Bring a friend—if you have one." Churchill replied that he had other commitments on the night in question and asked Shaw to send tickets for the second performance—if there was one.[3] At a dinner party, Nancy Astor said to Churchill,

"Winston, if I were married to you, I'd put poison in your coffee." Churchill's reply: "Nancy, if you were my wife, I'd drink it."[4] On another occasion, politician Bessie Braddock scolded Churchill for being drunk. Churchill's reply: "Indeed, Madam, and you are ugly, but tomorrow I'll be sober."[5] What makes these insults so clever is the way Churchill creates a variant of the original insult and throws it back at the insulter.

The ability to engage in repartee, I should add, is sufficiently rare that it can confer a kind of immortality on a person. It also confers a kind of immortality on the recipient of his comeback: these days, Bessie Braddock is remembered—when she is remembered at all—as one of the people who tried, unsuccessfully, to insult Winston Churchill.

Another comeback artist was Cynic philosopher Diogenes, who lived in the fourth century BC. A financial scandal had forced Diogenes to flee Sinope. When someone brought up this incident from his past in order to shame him, Diogenes responded that although it was true that the people of Sinope had sentenced him to exile, he in turn had sentenced them to remain in Sinope.[6] Diogenes was also apparently a master of the so-called chiastic counterinsult, in which the insulted person responds by changing the order of the words in the insult. Thus, when Aristippus chided Diogenes for his simple lifestyle—"If you would only learn to flatter the king, you wouldn't have to live on lentils"—Diogenes replied that if Aristippus would only learn to live on lentils, he wouldn't have to flatter the king.[7]

ANOTHER WAY TO RESPOND to an insult—useful to those of us not likely to go down in history for our skillful repartee—is by dismissing it. In doing this, we don't offer a counterinsult. We don't ignore the insult either. Instead, we make it clear to the insulter that the insult has failed to damage its target.

One way to dismiss an insult is by instantly forgiving it. Suppose the insulter calls us a blathering idiot. We might respond as follows: "You have insulted me, but not to worry: all is forgiven." If he insults us again, we might tell him, "Go ahead and insult me if you feel you must. Get it out of your system. Really, I'm glad to be of service." This kind of forgiveness can be profoundly unsettling to the insulter. Here he is, assaulting us with insults, and we are taking the pummeling like a good Christian: we are turning the other cheek. If there are bystanders during this exchange, this can have the effect of making the insulter look petty and mean, and the victim of the insult wise and self-possessed. Thus the victim can exact revenge while seeming to take the moral high ground.

Alternatively, we can dismiss an insult by transforming it into a joke. This is what Roman politician and statesman Cato the Younger did when Lentulus, a legal adversary, spit in his face. After calmly wiping off the spittle, Cato said, "I will swear to anyone, Lentulus, that people are wrong to say that you cannot use your mouth!"[8] In the twentieth century, writer Gore Vidal used a clever variant of this comeback. The story goes that he had insulted Norman Mailer's writing, and Mailer had responded by punching him. As Vidal was getting up off the floor, he commented that "Once again, words have failed Norman."[9]

We can also dismiss an insult by thanking the person who insulted us. By doing this, we demonstrate to the insulter that her effort to insult us has failed, and we do it without unleashing a counterinsult. Suppose, for example, a colleague tells us that an article we wrote has lately been her favorite bedtime reading—and that reading it has put her to sleep three nights in a row. We might respond to this insult simply by saying, "Thanks." It is a response calculated to baffle the insulter: we did not fight back, as she had both hoped and expected; nor did the insult seem to give us any pain.

After the insulter recovers from her initial bafflement, she might respond to our thanks by abandoning the attempt to insult us. Or she might respond by explaining to us that we have been insulted—but of course, an insult you have to explain is like a joke you have to explain: both are flops. Furthermore, after the insulter explains to us that we have been insulted, it is pretty clear what we should say: "I know. Thanks." In most cases, one imagines, this response will silence her. (And what if it doesn't? What if she instead calls us a fool? Our reply is ready at hand: "Thanks!")

I have, during the course of my research on insults, experimented with the "Thanks" reply and have discovered not only that it is effective, but that in an interesting number of cases, an insulter will respond by attempting to retract her insult. In the hypothetical insult described above, for example, the insulter might say something like this: "Actually, I didn't mean to say that it was your article that put me to sleep. What I was trying to say is that I have been reading your paper at bedtime but have lately been too tired to get through much of it."

This response reveals how complex the psychology of insults is. In unleashing her insult, the insulter had wanted, presumably, to show the author of the article that she does not take him to be her intellectual superior or even her intellectual equal. At the same time, though, she doesn't want the author of the article to become an enemy as the result of having been insulted. When the insulted person says "Thanks," she worries that he has taken the insult personally, and so she retracts it.

Saying "Thanks" in response to an insult has many advantages. It is an easy response to remember, it can be used in a wide range of circumstances, it doesn't require wit, and best of all, it robs the insulter of the pleasure she might have taken in insulting us. Indeed, the "Thanks" response is likely to leave the insulter thoroughly frustrated.

THE DISMISSIVE RESPONSES described above deal with an insult by shrugging it off. We thereby demonstrate to the insulter that his insult did not hurt us. In another kind of dismissive response, we dismiss not just the insult but the insulter as well. In doing this, we don't attack the insulter personally, the way we would in a retaliatory insult. Instead, we imply that because he is who he is, the things he says to us can have little or no effect on us.

One way to dismiss an insulter is by exploring with him his motives for insulting us. Thus, if someone calls us a fool, we might respond by asking whether he is in a bad mood. Or if, after we have been awarded some honor, a coworker tells us that our winning it is evidence that the standards for awarding the honor in question have fallen, we might respond by asking whether our success makes him uncomfortable, or more aggressively, whether he feels threatened by our success, and more aggressively still, whether he envies us for winning the award.

(Posing the question in this last manner, I might add, will likely jeopardize our relationship with this person, especially if he *does* envy us.) By examining the insulter's motives, we are implying that he is insulting us because of his own personal shortcomings—because he is given to mood swings, say, or is insecure—and that we are therefore justified in dismissing his views.

Notice that in analyzing the insulter's motives, we aren't so much criticizing his insulting behavior as excusing it: we are attributing his insults to something in his personality over which he has little control. I should add that the insulter probably won't enjoy having his motives analyzed: the insult is supposed to be about us, not about him! Nor will he appreciate our trying to find an excuse for his behavior: curiously, he wants his behavior to be inexcusable, not that he is likely to come out and say as much. This is the thing to realize about dismissive responses: they can cause an insulter considerably more discomfort than a direct insult would.

Here is an experiment for readers to try: the next time someone insults you, ask, "Why did you say that?" It is a response that is likely to stop the insulter in his tracks. It is also likely to lessen the chances that he will insult you again in the future. Most people, after all, will go to great lengths to avoid self-examination.

We can also dismiss an insulter by calling into question not his psychological makeup but his values. Suppose that on hearing that we have a certain goal, someone tells us that we are wasting our time to pursue it. In making this statement, the insulter is revealing that he has different values than we do. If we are confident that our values are correct and his are mistaken, we can reply that we are glad he feels this way, the implication being that if *he* thinks a goal isn't worth pursuing, we can be confident that it *is* worth pursuing.

There are, I might add, people who feel threatened whenever it becomes apparent that someone else's values differ from their own. Thus, if we own a different kind of car, live in a different neighborhood, or have a different vocation than they do, they will take it as evidence that we disapprove of their choice of car, neighborhood, and vocation. They will feel insulted, and they will take revenge on us by insulting our own choices in these matters. (Realize that from the point of view of these individuals, the insults they direct at us are not first-strike insults; to the contrary, they are retaliatory insults, triggered by our implied disapproval of their values.) The individuals in question will do this, I should add, even though we have never made a disparaging remark about their choices—indeed, even though we have praised their choices.

It is in large part because we don't like having our values challenged that we tend, in our social lives, to sort ourselves into groups that share similar values. This way, when we socialize, we will be unlikely to spend our time insulting each other; we can instead spend it rather more enjoyably, insulting those individuals who are foolish enough not to share our preferences in cars, neighborhoods, or occupations. Meanwhile, of course, the people we insult will be off in their own social groups, saying insulting things about us.

A MORE AGGRESSIVE WAY to dismiss an insulter is by saying, "Whatever." In saying this, we are implying that we don't really care what the insulter thinks, that his feelings are irrelevant. It was this response that allegedly triggered an outburst of anger in actor Russell Crowe. He had been unable to reach his wife on a hotel phone. When he called the hotel's concierge to complain, the concierge responded, "Whatever," and on hearing this, Crowe threaten to come down and "kick his ass." Subsequently, he did go down, but instead of kicking the concierge, Crowe threw a phone at him. It was an assault that could conceivably have put Crowe behind bars for eight years.[10] Such is the power of a dismissive response. People just don't appreciate being dismissed.

It is possible, by the way, to make the "Whatever" response even more annoying by truncating it to "Whatev." It is presumably a good thing that the abovementioned concierge didn't do this.

Let us consider one final and, some would say, ultimately dismissive reply. Suppose, once again, that someone calls us a blathering idiot and we respond by saying, "What makes you think I care what you think about me? What you think simply doesn't matter." You might imagine that someone who regards us as a blathering idiot would have no interest at all in our opinion of him, but you would be quite mistaken. Indeed, declaring our utter contempt for an individual is the ultimate insult, for as Lord Chesterfield explained to his son, "Wrongs are often forgiven, but contempt never is. Our pride remembers it forever."[11] To dismiss someone in the manner just described is, in the war of insults, the equivalent of a nuclear strike.

So far, we have considered verbal responses to insults, including some that are quite aggressive. It is also possible, of course, to respond to an insult not with words but with actions: when insulted, we might physically attack the insulter. There are doubtless circumstances in which it makes sense to respond in a physical manner to a verbal insult. In particular, prison inmates who do not respond forcefully to insults can find that they become the equivalent of another prisoner's slave—his bitch, as they say in prison. And in some cultures, it makes sense to respond to an insult by challenging someone to a duel—makes sense, that is, if one wishes to retain one's way of life. By way of illustration, historian Ute Frevert reports that in Germany in the early eighteenth century, "to be regarded as a coward for avoiding a duel equaled expulsion from society, a social death sentence, to which possible death in a duel was obviously preferable."[12] Thus, if someone insulted a university student and he didn't respond by challenging the insulter to a duel, the insulted individual became a marked man, the target of his peers' insults: they would rudely repeat the insult to him, and they would refuse to talk, eat, or drink with him.[13]

In those cultures that condoned dueling, people generally had a heightened sense of honor. In Italy in the late nineteenth century, for example, reading someone's newspaper without his permission might make him feel sufficiently insulted that he would challenge the reader to a duel.[14] And in Amsterdam in the early eighteenth century, kicking someone's dog was grounds for a duel—especially if, after being kicked, the dog toppled his owner's pot of beer.[15]

In some cultures, if a woman was seduced, one of her male relatives might challenge her seducer to a duel. It is worth noting, though, that his goal in doing this wasn't to restore the woman's honor; that would have been irretrievably lost. Instead, his goal would have been to restore his own honor.[16] In other cultures, if a man's daughter was seduced, the man might restore his honor not by dueling the seducer but by committing an "honor killing"—of the daughter, by stoning her to death.

Significantly, the codes of honor that condoned dueling usually applied only to gentlemen. Thus, if one gentleman killed another in a duel, the law looked the other way, but if a laborer killed another laborer in a fair fight, the law counted him a murderer.[17] Also, contrary to popular belief, for a duel to restore honor it wasn't necessary for someone to die; in many cultures, all that was required was a nonfatal shedding of blood.[18] The mere fact that someone was willing to take part in a duel was proof, people thought, that he was courageous and honorable.

What do you do if you have a heightened sense of honor but live in a society that has banned dueling? Instead of challenging the person who has dishonored you to a duel, you might, without any ceremony, assault him. There are, of course, problems with this manner of response. To begin with, the person you attack might be bigger and stronger than you are: yes, you punched him in the nose for calling you a name, but he subsequently broke both your legs. Furthermore, the law will punish you for attacking him: you punched him in the nose, but the legal system not only put you in jail for doing so but awarded him damages against you.

Having said this, I should add that even those societies that have outlawed dueling and that frown on physical violence in response to verbal insults have exceptions. In particular, if a verbal insult amounts to what is known as "fighting words," you might not be incarcerated for punching the insulter. We will take a closer look at fighting words in the next chapter.

So FAR IN THIS CHAPTER, we have talked about doing *something* in response to an insult—stinging an insulter with a witty reply, perhaps, or punching him in the nose. It is also possible, though, to respond to an insult by doing absolutely nothing. Someone can, in other words, practice *insult pacifism*.

A *pacifist* in the normal sense of the word is a person who refuses to respond to violence with violence. Hit him and he will not hit you back; indeed, he might turn the other cheek so you can hit him again. Correspondingly, an *insult pacifist* is a person who refuses to respond to verbal violence with verbal violence: he will not respond to an insult with a counterinsult. Furthermore, an insult pacifist will be unwilling to unleash first-strike insults, the way a pacifist in the usual sense of the word will be unwilling to strike a first blow.

Suppose, then, that someone calls an insult pacifist lazy. He might respond to this insult with no response at all; he might, in other words, carry on as if nothing had been said. Indeed, even when an insult is physical rather than verbal, a pacifist might do nothing in response. Thus, when someone struck Cato (who seems to have been subject to more than his share of physical abuse) at the public baths, he did nothing in response, and when that person, on realizing who Cato was, came up to apologize, Cato simply said that he didn't remember being struck.[19] Why not accept the apology? Because he refused to acknowledge that he had been wronged by the action. "He showed finer spirit in not acknowledging" the insult, observed Stoic philosopher Seneca, "than if he had pardoned it."[20]

The Stoics, by the way, did not invent insult pacifism. Indeed, as we saw in chapter 1, as far back as the Old Testament, we can find elements of pacifism: the Book of Proverbs informs us that "a clever man slighted conceals his feelings." The Stoics are notable, though, for being the first (to my knowledge) to recommend pacifism as the default response to almost every insult.

It should by now be clear that insult pacifism is the easiest to use of the insult-response strategies we have considered. Not everyone is witty enough to respond to an insult with a clever counterinsult, and not everyone can successfully memorize a bunch of faux-witty counterinsults to use in self-defense, should the occasion arise. Even someone in a coma, though, can practice pacifism: when insulted, he will make no response, and his insulter, one hopes, will quickly tire of insulting him.

SOMETIMES, RATHER THAN REMAIN SILENT in the face of an insult, an insult pacifist will feel compelled to say *something* in response. His pacifism does not allow him to respond to an insult with a verbal attack on his insulter, but it does allow him to respond with a verbal attack on himself. He can, more precisely, respond to an insult with a self-deprecating remark. Suppose, once again, that someone accuses the pacifist of being lazy. He might respond by admitting to this failing: "Sadly, what you say is true." The thing to realize is that the pacifist might do this even though he thinks himself a rather industrious individual.

It can be useful, when engaging in self-deprecation, to add an element of humor—to make a joke, that is, at our own expense. (This, it should be noted, is different from the technique of making a joke *at the insulter's expense,* as Cato did when Lentulus spit in his face.) Thus, a self-deprecating pacifist, after admitting his laziness, might give his confession a comical spin: "To be perfectly honest with you, though, this particular failing of mine wouldn't even make it onto my own top-five list of personal shortcomings."

For another example of self-deprecating humor, consider Vatinius, a man whose neck was covered with wens and whose feet were diseased. Vatinius, says Seneca, told so many jokes about his own deformities that others had nothing to add.[21] Another (albeit fictional) example of self-deprecating humor can be found in Edmund Rostand's *Cyrano de Bergerac.* When someone attempts to insult Cyrano by telling him that his nose is big, Cyrano responds by asking, "Is that all?" When the insulter is puzzled by this response, Cyrano goes on to provide a long list of insults of his nose that are superior to the one the insulter has used.

Besides using self-deprecation in response to malicious insults, insult pacifists might use it in response to the benign insults described in chapter 5. If, for example, a pacifist's spouse playfully teases him—"You are such a pack rat!"—he might respond by correcting her: "Actually, I'm more of a rat-pig hybrid—on steroids." Likewise, if his friends tease him as part of a test to see whether he thinks he is socially superior to them—

to see, for example, whether a recent promotion has gone to his head—he might respond with self-deprecation; by doing so, he will reassure them that he remains "one of them."

And while we are on the topic of playful teasing, let me point out that although an insult pacifist will refrain from inflicting malicious first-strike insults, he might be perfectly willing to inflict playful insults, both in a first-strike manner and in response to being playfully insulted. He will realize that such insults perform an important role in building and maintaining social relationships. Even the Stoics, who were staunch advocates of insult pacifism, seemed to have allowed playful teasing. Indeed, this is probably what Stoic philosopher Musonius Rufus was doing when he referred to Epictetus, who had been a slave before becoming Musonius's student, as "slave" during classroom discussions.[22] At the same time, he will take great care in his use of such insults, since he will appreciate how easy it is to cross the line between insults that are genuinely playful and insults that may seem playful but that in fact contain a malicious element.

Another thing an insult pacifist might do in response to an insult is announce that he is a pacifist and then explain to the insulter what insult pacifism is. Alternatively, he might respond, not with a lecture about insult pacifism, but with an apology: "Sorry, but I don't do insults."

ON HEARING THE ABOVE DESCRIPTION of insult pacifism, readers will naturally wonder whether it is an effective way to deal with insults. They will therefore be reluctant to practice pacifism.

An advocate of pacifism might try to reassure them by pointing out, to begin with, that nearly all of us *sometimes* practice pacifism in response to insults. Suppose, for example, that while we are walking down the street, a stranger shouts out that we are a stupid fathead. It is quite sensible, under these circumstances, to do absolutely nothing in response—to walk on as if nothing had been said. Likewise, if it is our boss rather than a stranger who calls us a stupid fathead, we would do well to hold our tongue and carry on as if nothing has happened. In other words, we *already* practice pacifism; the advocate of insult pacifism is merely recommending that we expand this practice and make it our standard response to *all* insults.

Those who hear this recommendation will likely respond that the cases just described are special. In the case of the stranger, we don't need to respond forcefully because we know we will never have to deal with him again. And in the case of our boss, we *can't* respond forcefully, at least not if we want to keep our job. But suppose it isn't a stranger or our boss who insults us, but an acquaintance, neighbor, teammate, or coworker. We will, under these circumstances, find it hard to do nothing in response to this insult and harder still to do nothing if the insult takes place in front of a group of people with whom we will have dealings in the future. We will worry that if we respond to the insult with pacifism, the insulter and those who witness his insult will regard us as a safe target for insults and will therefore pummel us with them in the future. This concern will stand between many people and the practice of insult pacifism.

Is this concern justified? Is it true that insult pacifists will find themselves deluged with insults? I have, in recent years, paid attention to other people's use of insult pacifism and have experimented with it myself. I have discovered that pacifism in response to insults isn't nearly as risky as one might think.

How do insulters respond to pacifism? What do they do when, on insulting someone, he responds with self-deprecation or by doing nothing at all? In most cases, they respond with befuddlement. They aren't used to pacifism. To the contrary, they expect an insult to be met with a rebuttal or a counterinsult. Respond in either manner, and they know what to do next: either rebut the rebuttal or counter the counterinsult. But if you respond with pacifism, they are left scratching their head.

Suppose, for example, that a pacifist does absolutely nothing in response to an insult: he carries on as if nothing had been said. The insulter might initially suspect that he is not responding because he didn't hear the insult or misheard what she said. Or perhaps she will conclude that he heard what she said but is too thickheaded to realize that he has been insulted. She might, in either of these cases, feel compelled to repeat the insult. And if, in response to this repetition, he remains silent or says "I heard what you said the first time," her bafflement will grow. Not only that, but she will find herself frustrated by this response. She had intended to hurt him, discomfit him, or at least to have fun at his expense. Her plan has obviously failed miserably.

In saying that insulters are frustrated by their encounters with insult pacifists, I am speaking from personal experience. I have, in the past, insulted people who turned out to be pacifists.

Their nonresponse to my insult left me feeling foolish. Indeed, the experience was sufficiently unpleasant that on determining that someone was a pacifist, I rarely insulted him a second time; instead, I put him on my mental do-not-insult list.

As further evidence of the effectiveness of pacifism, consider that some of the world's greatest insulters were defeated by it. Samuel Johnson was skilled at repartee: he liked to insult others and, when they attempted to reply, top their response. Occasionally, Johnson would encounter someone who refused to play the insult game, and he found such encounters to be profoundly unsatisfying: "I hate a fellow whom pride, or cowardice, or laziness drives into a corner, and who does nothing when he is there but sit and *growl*; let him come out as I do, and *bark*."[23] Much the same can be said of George Bernard Shaw. He once published an attack on G. K. Chesterton's economic views. Chesterton chose not to respond, and when asked why, he said, "I *have* answered him. To a man of Shaw's wit, silence is the one unbearable repartee."[24]

And if a pacifist responds to an insult not with silence but with self-deprecation, an insulter is likely to be even more frustrated. When she insulted him, he not only didn't fight back but insulted himself even worse than she had done. And if his self-deprecation contains an element of humor, things are worse still: the insulter will be disheartened to realize that her verbal punch left her target laughing. His self-deprecation makes it painfully clear to the insulter that he is immune to her insults and that she is therefore wasting her time by trying to insult him.

And finally, if a pacifist responds to an insult by declaring himself to be an insult pacifist, she is likely to be astonished. It will probably come as news to her that someone can be a pacifist with respect to insults. As soon as she recovers from her initial astonishment, though, she might put his pacifism to the test by bombarding him with insults to see whether she can provoke him into hurling one back. As long as he keeps shrugging his shoulders in response—"Sorry, but like I said, I don't do insults"—she will ultimately grow weary and try to seek out an easier target for her put-downs.

After her encounter with the pacifist, the insulter might find that she feels vaguely insulted by his behavior. In refusing to inflict or respond to insults, he is implying that he is above this sort of thing, that he has outgrown insults. The implication, of course, is that she has not outgrown them, an implication she will likely resent. She might also try to convince herself that she hadn't wronged the pacifist: "I wasn't insulting him; I was just talking to him. He must be hypersensitive or something."

More generally, it isn't unusual for an insulter to blame her victim for failing to take offense at being insulted. On one occasion, after I had resorted to self-deprecating humor in response to an attack on my character, my insulter responded by turning her attention to another perceived character flaw: "You should take things more seriously!" she complained.

It is possible for an insulter, after encountering an insult pacifist, to become aware of her own insulting tendencies, and this might lead her to reassess the way she behaves toward other people. It is thus possible for insult pacifists to trigger a social epiphany in the insulters they encounter. (This can also happen when violent people encounter, for the first time, a person who is pacifistic in the normal sense of the word: it can open their eyes to their own violent nature.) It is also possible, of course, for insulters, on encountering a pacifist, to walk away puzzled but with their insulting tendencies fully intact.

AT THIS POINT, readers might remain unconvinced by the argument for practicing pacifism in response to insults. They might have encountered insulters who, when not dealt with forcefully by the target of an insult, went on an insult rampage. A decade ago, for example, they might have failed to respond forcefully to an insult directed at them by their loutish neighbor. This same individual might, as a consequence, bombard them with insults every time he encounters them. And because he is so busy insulting them during these encounters, he remains oblivious to the fact that his insults are being conspicuously ignored. Insult pacifism, they might conclude, is powerless against such an individual.

These readers should realize that those who advocate insult pacifism are not only aware of such cases but have a strategy for dealing with them. In particular, the Stoics—who, as we have seen, favored pacifism in response to insults—realized that there are adults who, despite their years, remain children, mentally and emotionally speaking.[25] And in the same way as a mother would admonish or punish a misbehaving child, we should, says Stoic philosopher Seneca, admonish or punish the slow-witted lout who childishly keeps insulting us. When we do so, though, we need to remember that we are doing it not for our own good and certainly not to settle a score; to the contrary, we are doing it for the good of the person who insulted us.[26] We are attempting to train him—to teach him proper social behavior.

IN THE ABOVE DISCUSSION of insult pacifism, I focused my attention on the pacifist's external response to insults: he will behave as if the insult has had no effect on him. For him to be able to do this, though, it is important that he remain calm internally in the face of an insult. If he is angered by an insult, after all, it is likely that he will respond to it not with silence or self-deprecation, but with retaliation.

Thus, an insult pacifist, while working on his external response to insults, will want also to work on his internal response. He will want to put himself into a frame of mind that prevents insults from upsetting him. If he can accomplish this, his failure to respond to an insult will not simply be a show put on for the benefit of the world around him; it will instead be a true reflection of how he feels about the insult. In other words, a pacifist will strive to become a person who, besides seeming to be immune to insults, is in fact immune to them.

I realize that this sounds like quite an undertaking, but in chapter 11, I will offer readers some advice, derived from the Stoics, on how to accomplish this goal. Before doing this, however, allow me, in the next chapter, to complete my discussion of responses to insults. So far, we have considered what I termed personal responses—namely, the things individuals can do in response to an insult. Let us, in the next chapter, consider societal responses—namely, the steps societies can take to minimize the harm done by insults.

CHAPTER 10

Societal Responses to Insults

IN THE PREVIOUS CHAPTER, we examined the ways individuals can deal with insults—with a witty comeback, for example, or with silence. Let us now turn our attention to the ways in which society can deal with insults.

In what follows, I will be using *society* in a broad sense of the word. Thus, among the societal responses to insults I consider will be the actions of governments (which might, for example, outlaw slander or hate speech), nongovernmental institutions such as corporations (which might chastise or terminate an employee for insulting someone), and universities (which might adopt speech codes that forbid certain insulting language). One of the most important ways society attempts to deal with insults, though, is by adopting codes of politeness, and it is to these codes that we will now turn our attention.

STRICTLY SPEAKING, societies don't *adopt* codes of politeness: there isn't a big convention at which etiquette experts gather to devise and enact a code. Instead, these codes arise spontaneously. Furthermore, within a particular society, the code of politeness can evolve with the passage of time, so that one generation's idea of good manners horrifies the previous generation, whose own code of politeness was radically different.

In the society in which I live, the code of politeness requires me to do certain things under certain circumstances. It requires me (or at least used to require me—our code of politeness has changed dramatically over the course of my life) to open doors for women and old people; to cover my mouth when I sneeze; not to wipe my nose on my sleeve; not to swear around women and children; to send a thank-you note after receiving a gift and send it in a timely manner; to return a greeting; to shake another person's hand when it is offered; not to wear a hat in a church or go bareheaded in a synagogue; not to ask others how much money they make; and not to burp at the dinner table. If I violate these or any of the other directives of my society's code of politeness, those around me will think (or, in days gone by, would have thought) me rude.

There was presumably a time, at the dawn of humanity, when codes of politeness didn't exist. But according to sociologist Norbert Elias, as human groups became bigger and interactions, especially with nonrelatives, became more commonplace, codes of politeness became important: "People, forced to live with one another in a new way, become more sensitive to the impulses of others. Not abruptly but very gradually the code of behavior becomes stricter and the degree of consideration expected from others becomes greater. The sense of what to do and what not to do in order not to offend or shock others becomes subtler, and in conjunction with the new power relationships the social imperative not to offend others becomes more binding."[1]

Although we don't know when the first code of politeness came into existence, we know that such codes have been around for a very long time. They are also ubiquitous: all cultures have them. At the same time, the codes of different cultures typically vary, for the simple reason that the choice of what behavior counts as polite is rather arbitrary. If we all agreed that belching at those you meet counted as polite behavior, then belching under these circumstances would be polite; it might instead be saying "Hi" to those you meet that was considered rude.

THE MOST IMPORTANT FUNCTION of a code of politeness is to give a society guidelines on what does and doesn't count as insulting behavior. Having such guidelines, after all, makes it easier to settle social disputes—makes it easier, that is, to determine who is to blame when someone thinks she has been insulted. In some cases, the person who feels insulted will be right: the person who offended her has indeed violated her society's code of politeness and is therefore to blame for the dispute. In other cases, the person who feels insulted will be in the wrong: the person who offended her will have acted in accordance with the code of politeness, meaning that it is the person who feels insulted who is to blame for the dispute.

In the absence of a code of politeness, what counts as insulting behavior is subjective: insults will be in the mind of the beholder. As a result, there will be a lot more people who feel that they have been insulted and a lot more people who are surprised that someone found their behavior to be insulting. Under such circumstances, social disputes will be difficult to settle, and this will cause needless strain on the social fabric.

Having a code of politeness dramatically simplifies daily living. Suppose we didn't have such a code, and I saw you walking toward me on the street. If I didn't want to insult you, I would have to analyze the situation carefully. How sensitive a person are you? How did you behave during previous encounters? What can I say or do to avoid offending you? If we have a shared code of politeness, though, such analysis is unnecessary. I need only say "Hi"—or, here in the Midwest, where I live, say "Hey." If you are offended by this, the problem is yours, not mine. Thus, as Emerson reminds us, "Manners aim to facilitate life."[2]

Ironically, codes of politeness, besides telling us how to avoid insulting others, provide us with a blueprint of what, exactly, we should do if our goal is to insult them. For example, in our society, we can reliably insult most people by failing to shake their hand when they extend it. If a society lacked a code of politeness, though, insulting others would be rather more challenging. We could not exploit the code of politeness as a source of ready-made insults; we would instead, if we wished to insult someone, have to study him and custom-design an insult that, because of his personality and values, would be likely to offend him.

IN THE LATE 1970S, in America and elsewhere, codes of politeness were supplemented with another kind of code, one that specified what kind of speech was likely to be insulting to members of certain disadvantaged groups. The code in question—let us call it the *PC code*, short for the *political correctness code*—declared, among other things, that instead of calling someone a *Negro*—a term that might offend him—we should call him *black*, and that instead of calling someone *crippled*, we should call her *handicapped*.

The PC code plays a role parallel to that played by politeness codes. A code of politeness tells what we must and must not do if we wish to be regarded as well-mannered; the PC code tells what we must and must not say if we wish to be regarded as unprejudiced. In much the same way as those who support codes of politeness will go out of their way to learn proper manners—will learn, for example, which eating utensils to use at a formal dinner—those who support the PC code will go out of their way to learn the currently accepted labels for people who belong to various disadvantaged groups. And in the same way as those who have taken time to master the politeness code will be proud of their accomplishment and might feel justified in correcting those who behave rudely, those who master the PC code likewise might feel proud of having done so and might take it upon themselves to correct those around them who engage in politically incorrect speech.

Despite these parallels, we should not make the mistake of thinking that anyone who supports politeness codes also supports the PC code, or conversely. Those who support politeness codes are interested in fostering a civil society, one in which good manners are the norm. Those who support PC codes are interested in fostering a society free of prejudice. It is entirely possible, though, for someone to be antiprejudice without being pro-good manners, and conversely. For this reason, one periodically encounters people who are scrupulous when it comes to obeying the PC code but who have little regard for codes of politeness: the rudeness of these individuals does not prevent them from being deeply offended on hearing, for example, someone use the word "crippled" to refer to a person in a wheelchair. Likewise, one periodically encounters exceptionally well-mannered bigots.

Those who formulated the PC code soon made an interesting discovery. They advised us to call someone in a wheelchair *handicapped* rather than *crippled* because some of those we called *crippled* would take it as an insult. The problem is that by focusing people's attention on what others called them, they sensitized people to insults. Indeed, before long, the terms sanctioned by the PC code themselves started sounding like insults: in particular, some of those in wheelchairs started to resent being called *handicapped*. As a result, the guardians of the PC code were forced to come up with a new term to replace *handicapped*. They settled on *disabled*, only to discover, once again, that this failed to mollify those to whom they wished to apply the word. As a result, they jettisoned *disabled* in favor of *differently abled*—and for all I know, even this last term has fallen out of favor. All it takes is for someone, somewhere to object to the adjective the PC code has assigned to him, and the search for the perfect euphemism must begin anew.

For another example of this phenomenon, consider the search for a politically correct term for people of African ancestry. In 1906, the National Negro Committee was founded, but it soon renamed itself the National Association for the Advancement of Colored People, or NAACP. (*Negro* is, after all, uncomfortably reminiscent of the n-word.) In the 1960s, the term *colored person* was abandoned—by most people, but not by the NAACP—in favor of *black*. In the 1980s, *black* was, for many people, replaced by *Afro-American*. It didn't take long, though, for someone to point out that the Afro is a hair style, so that calling someone an Afro-American is offensive, inasmuch as it implies that all Afro-Americans have Afros. For this reason, *Afro-American* mutated into *African American*. By the 1990s, even *African American* came to be regarded as vaguely insulting and was supplanted by *people of color*. From *colored people* to *people of color* in just under a century—the chain of euphemisms had nearly succeeded in catching its own tail!

WHEN THE PC MOVEMENT gained momentum, its advocates were able to put teeth into political correctness. It wasn't enough, they thought, simply to chastise those who used politically incorrect terminology; instead, such people should be punished. They encouraged American corporations to develop policies that prohibited language that employees who were members of certain disadvantaged groups might find insulting. They also encouraged American universities to develop speech codes that prohibited certain kinds of speech on campus. In 1990, for example, Stanford University adopted a speech code that forbids speech "intended to insult or stigmatize an individual or a small number of individuals on the basis of their sex, race, color, handicap, religion, sexual orientation, or national and ethnic origin."[3] On the Stanford campus, it was still permissible to call your roommate stupid, but you had better not call her a stupid woman, stupid Catholic, or stupid Italian.

These speech codes doubtless reduced the number of racial and ethnic slurs heard on America's college campuses—a good thing. But in the process of doing so, they also inhibited free speech in what used to be some of the intellectually freest places on the planet. Professors and students alike realized that because of speech codes, they had better be careful of what they said in the presence of others. Obviously, they shouldn't make disparaging remarks about those in disadvantaged groups—they shouldn't, for example, call an Italian a wop.

But besides this, they had to be careful not to say something that, although it didn't directly insult members of a disadvantaged group, might nevertheless displease them. It became unwise, for example, to question the efficacy of affirmative action programs, the goal of which was to benefit members of these groups. It similarly became unwise to question the efficacy of the political correctness movement—by suggesting, perhaps, that rather than reducing prejudice in our society, the movement only made it harder to spot the bigots among us. And ironically, it became unwise to question the appropriateness of campus speech codes. If you did any of these things and someone complained—or even worse, someone accused you of racism or sexism—you were likely in serious trouble.

Campus speech codes conferred considerable power on the most sensitive individual in each classroom—the one who was quickest to label something as being sexist or racist. That person, simply by feeling offended, could effectively control classroom discussions. Consider, by way of illustration, the case of adjunct professor Ken Hardy, who taught a course on interpersonal communication at a community college in

Kentucky. In a classroom discussion, he asked students for examples of insulting terms. One offered the word *nigger*. The class had twenty-two students, nine of whom were black. One of those black students objected to the use—more precisely, the mere mention—of this word. Hardy took this objection seriously and suggested that his students should as well. Nevertheless, he was subsequently fired, apparently for allowing *nigger* to be discussed in class and thereby offending a single student.[4]

In response to such cases, professors will understandably self-censor. When giving their lectures, they will consider the possibility that one of the students sitting before them has been hypersensitized by the PC movement. They will avoid saying anything that might offend this student, if he or she is indeed out there. As a result, in the process of demanding that classroom speech be politically correct, America's universities have had to relinquish a degree of intellectual freedom. Many advocates of political correctness, though, aren't bothered by this tradeoff: to their way of thinking, the ideas that can no longer be expressed in America's classrooms are not worth expressing.

BESIDES ADOPTING codes of politeness, societies typically adopt legal codes. These codes, like codes of politeness, are implemented in part to deal with insulting behavior, and like codes of politeness, they vary. Thus, the legal codes of some nations prohibit citizens from insulting divine beings, or religious or political leaders: in Thailand, for example, insulting the king can result in a lengthy jail sentence.[5] Under American law, by way of contrast, citizens are free to insult religious and political figures. It is likewise legal for them to insult—verbally, at any rate—their fellow citizens. If, for example, I walk up to a stranger and say, "Your haircut makes me want to barf," the police will not act to protect the feelings of the person I have insulted.

The legal system turns a blind eye to such insults in part because it has better things to do. And even if it had the resources to deal with such insults, it would refrain from doing so on the grounds that freedom of speech—which is protected by the First Amendment of the US Constitution—requires, among other things, that individuals be allowed to say things about other people that they don't want to hear. In other words, freedom of speech includes the freedom to insult others.

The First Amendment does not, however, grant Americans unlimited freedom to insult. An American had better not, for example, make insulting remarks to the judge during a court proceeding—he will be charged with contempt of court if he does. And in many municipalities, he will be punished if he insults a police officer. American law also prohibits insults in which someone says something false about someone else, if what he says damages her reputation. Suppose, for example, that someone announces, in front of an audience, that a coworker got promoted only because she slept with the boss. The coworker will doubtless feel insulted and might seek legal redress. In particular, she might sue the insulter for slander. (And if he instead made the accusation in a written document, she would sue him for libel.)

While proscribing some insults, the American legal system specifically allows others. In particular, American copyright laws protect insults in which someone mocks someone else's creative output. Suppose, for example, someone writes a parody of a short story. The parody might cut the story's author to the quick and might even hurt his literary reputation, but he is, in the American legal system, barred from suing the parodist for any emotional or financial damage his parody might have caused.

The American legal system, besides prohibiting certain insults, prohibits certain responses to insults. It prohibits, for example, dueling in response to a perceived slight. More generally, it prohibits a person from responding to a verbal insult with physical violence—unless, that is, the insult in question constitutes "fighting words." In that case, the legal system might punish the person who unleashed the insult, but not the person who responded to it with violence. Allow me to explain.

Suppose that instead of walking up to a stranger on the street and criticizing his haircut, I walk up and call him a chicken. Suppose that when he ignores me, I follow him down the street, repeatedly calling him a chicken, making clucking noises, and shouting out to passersby that the target of my abuse is a big chicken. Insulting him in this manner is, from a legal point of view,[6] tantamount to challenging him to fight me, meaning that if he turns around and punches me squarely in the nose, I will only be getting what I want—and deserve. Thus, if a policeman comes along at this point, he might dismiss the man who punched me. And after doing so, he might arrest me for using language likely to provoke violence.

IN RECENT DECADES, American lawmakers—spurred on, in part, by the political correctness movement—have taken an interest in those insults that involve the subcategory of politically incorrect language known as hate speech. In the insults in question, the insulter derogates members of a certain group for being members of that group. Thus, if I call a black person a stupid black (or even worse, if I employ the n-word in this insult), I might be accused of hate speech. If, however, I had simply called the black person stupid—if, that is, I had refrained from adding the group reference that suggests that he is stupid because of his membership in the group—I would not be guilty of hate speech. Only some groups are protected under the hate-speech umbrella.[7] If, for example, I call a white man a stupid white man—or even a stupid honky—I will not be guilty of hate speech. This is because white males are not a protected group.

Some municipalities have passed laws against hate speech. In 1990, for example, St. Paul, Minnesota, passed the St. Paul Bias Motivated Crime Ordinance: "Whoever places on public or private property a symbol, object, appellation, characterization or graffiti, including, but not limited to, a burning cross or Nazi swastika, which one knows or has reasonable grounds to know arouses anger, alarm or resentment in others on the basis of race, color, creed, religion or gender commits disorderly conduct and shall be guilty of a misdemeanor."[8] So far, this and similar hate speech laws have not withstood challenges to their constitutionality, and it is therefore unlikely that America will adopt wide-ranging laws against hate speech anytime soon.[9]

In Canada, by way of contrast, hate speech laws have withstood legal challenges. Thus, in the early 1980s, Canadian high-school teacher James Keegstra made anti-Semitic remarks in his classroom, characterizing Jews as being, among other things, money-loving child-killers. These insults led to his being tried for a breach of Section 319(2) of the Canadian Criminal Code, which calls for the imprisonment, for up to two years, of anyone who, "by communicating statements, other than in private conversation, willfully promotes hatred against any identifiable group." The identifiable groups are defined as "any section of the public distinguished by colour, race, religion, ethnic origin or sexual orientation." The law does allow group insults under some circumstances—when, for example, you can establish that the insult happens to be true.

Keegstra's conviction was upheld by the Canadian Supreme Court, but in his dissenting opinion, Justice La Forest questioned the efficacy of hate speech laws. He pointed out that pre-Hitler Germany had laws against hate speech that were very much like those Canada now has, and that more than two hundred incidents of hate speech were prosecuted in accordance with those laws. But, writes La Forest, "as subsequent history so painfully testifies, this type of legislation proved ineffectual on the one occasion when there was a real argument for it. Indeed, there is some indication that the Nazis of pre-Hitler Germany shrewdly exploited their criminal trials in order to increase the size of their constituency. They used the trials as platforms to propagate their message."[10] He argued, in other words, that laws against hate speech can be manipulated and turned to the advantage of hateful speakers.

And La Forest isn't the only one to question the wisdom of Canadian hate speech laws. Legal scholar Kent Greenawalt describes a case in which it seems morally defensible—or maybe even morally obligatory—to engage in what these laws would classify as hate speech. He asks us to imagine that members of the South African Dutch Reformed Church move to Canada, where in their sermons, they preach that blacks, because they are descendants of Ham, are inferior to whites. Imagine too, he says, that they advocate the establishment of apartheid in Canada. Suppose that in response to this, an upstanding citizen starts phoning people to warn them about the presence, in their community, of this abhorrent religion.

According to Greenawalt, because this action is "likely to expose members and the group to hatred or contempt," it would appear to violate the Canadian law against hate speech, which, Greenawalt reminds us, "recognizes no defense of honest religious disagreement (or any other disagreement)." He adds that "unless Canadian courts are willing to swallow the principle that vigorous religious disagreement is always inappropriate over the telephone, this kind of case seems one in which the impairment of legitimate expression is very great."[11]

IF STOIC PHILOSOPHER Epictetus had been alive to watch the rise of hate speech laws and, more generally, the political correctness movement, he would have shaken his head in disbelief. According to him, the best way to spare people the pain of being insulted is not to change the world so that they never experience insults; it is instead to change people so that they are, in effect, immune to insults. And, Epictetus would add, until they change themselves in this manner, they will have little chance at happiness.

Some people, on hearing this, might reply that Epictetus wouldn't be talking this way if he were a member of a disadvantaged group—if, for example, he were the descendant of slaves or if he had a physical handicap. The problem with this reply is that Epictetus was both lame and a slave. It is therefore conceivable that we moderns—and in particular, the advocates of political correctness—can gain some important insights into how best to deal with insults by studying Epictetus and the other Stoic philosophers. It is for this reason that we will, in the following chapter, turn our attention to the Stoics.

CHAPTER 11

Insults: The Inner Game

In chapter 9, we explored our options in responding to an insult, but the responses we examined were external responses, observable by our insulter and anyone else who happened to witness the encounter. We might have responded to the insult, for example, with a witty counterinsult, by physically assaulting the insulter, or by carrying on as if nothing had happened.

What is arguably more important than our external response to an insult, though, is our internal response. Suppose, by way of illustration, that two individuals have the same external response to an insult: both might offer the same witty retort, or if they are insult pacifists, both might carry on as if nothing had happened. Even though their external response is identical, their internal response might be dramatically different: the first individual might remain calm in the face of the insult, while the second individual, although appearing calm, might in fact be seething with anger. The first individual's internal response is clearly preferable to that of the second. After all, our goal in dealing with insults should be not merely to make it look as if they did us no harm but to prevent them from doing us any harm. If we let an insult upset us, it will have done us harm.

Thus, a thoughtful person, when devising a strategy for responding to insults, will be concerned with her external response but even more concerned with her internal response. She will be concerned, that is, with her psychological response to insults, the part of her response that is invisible to others. In particular, she will devise a strategy for preventing herself from being upset by the insults she is likely to experience in daily living.

We have already encountered the ancient Stoic philosophers and examined their advice on the proper external response to insults: they were, as we have seen, advocates of insult pacifism. As it so happens, the Stoics also developed an internal-response strategy. It is to this strategy that we will now turn our attention.

MOST PEOPLE ARE UNHAPPY, the Stoics reasoned, because they have chosen the wrong values by which to live. In particular, they are unhappy because they value fame and fortune.

Not everyone, to be sure, seeks to be famous the way Elton John and Queen Elizabeth are. Usually, people are willing to settle for a lower degree of fame than this. Some might seek regional or local rather than global renown. And those of us who don't crave even local renown want to be well thought of by relatives, neighbors, and coworkers. We want them to love, admire, or at least respect us. We want them to look up at us on the social hierarchy rather than looking down on us.

And in seeking fortune, not everyone is angling to become as wealthy as, say, Bill Gates. But they are working very hard—

or at least are plotting with great ingenuity—so they can enjoy an affluent lifestyle. They want to wear expensive clothes, drive an expensive car, and live in a house that is not only big but is located in the right neighborhood and filled with the right furnishings.

Another thing to realize is that even though people seek both social status and affluence, their primary goal is to attain social status. A case can be made, in particular, that their pursuit of affluence is instrumental: they pursue it not for its own sake but because increased affluence will enhance their social standing.[1] Why, after all, do they want the clothes, the car, and the house they long for? In large part because attaining these things will impress other people. Indeed, if there were no one around to impress, few would feel driven to live a life of luxury, even if they could attain that luxury without having to work for it. Likewise, if wealthy individuals found themselves living in a culture in which people despised rather than admired those who live in luxury, one imagines that they would abandon their mansion and late-model Ferrari in favor of a modest home with an old Ford parked in the driveway.

In conclusion, people place great value on other people's opinions of them. Insults hurt so much because they are reminders that our social standing is not as high as we would like it to be. As we have seen, our preoccupation with social standing is a consequence of our evolutionary past. Fortunately for us, though, it is possible to override much of this evolutionary programming and thereby gain greater happiness and fulfillment. The first step in doing this is to reconsider our personal values.

IT IS UNUSUAL FOR PEOPLE to acquire their values through a process of careful reflection. Instead, they tend to take the easy way out and adopt whatever values those around them have adopted. And how did those around them choose their values? Probably by listening to their evolutionary programming. It rewards them for doing some things—having sex, for example, or gaining social status—and punishes them for doing other things. But this evolutionary programming, as we have seen, is not concerned with their having a happy and meaningful life; it is instead concerned with encouraging them to do things that, on the savannas of Africa 100,000 years ago, would have increased their chances of surviving and reproducing.

But we in developed nations are in a radically different environment than that of our evolutionary ancestors. As a result, we have the luxury of having as our goal not merely surviving and reproducing, but living a life that is both happy and meaningful. If we are to achieve this goal, though, we will have to take steps to circumvent, to some extent, our evolutionary programming: we will sometimes have to forgo opportunities for pleasure, and we will sometimes have to do things that we know will feel bad. And as part of this process, we will need to adopt values that are at odds with our evolutionary programming.

At the top of the list of the programming we should work to overcome (to the extent possible) is the programming that makes us care about our social standing. Unless we can do this, it is unlikely that we will escape from our evolutionary past. If, after all, we care what others think of us, we will find ourselves doing things calculated to please them, and the easiest way to accomplish this is by adopting and living in accordance with their values.

Notice, after all, that if we adopt values different from theirs, they will conclude that we reject their values, which will annoy them. They will also wonder whether we are justified in rejecting their values. If we are, it means that they will have to rethink their values, and this realization will further annoy them: if there is one thing people hate even worse than thinking, it is rethinking!

People will likely respond to the vexation we have caused them by making us the target of insults. If we care what they think of us, though, these insults will sting, and to make them stop, we need only abandon our unorthodox values. The people around us will then welcome us back into the fold and praise us for being so much like they are. (It is, after all, a socially acceptable way to praise themselves.) And because we care what they think about us, we will very much enjoy this praise. We will have learned an important lesson.

If, however, we adopt the values of the people around us, and if these people, because they are reluctant to examine the values by which they live, have chosen the wrong values, it means that we, too, will end up choosing the wrong values. We will, as a result, find ourselves joining the masses in their pursuit of fame and fortune. Doing this will win their approval, but will also jeopardize our chance of having a good and meaningful life. This, I think, is why the Stoic philosopher Epictetus warns us that "if people think you amount to something, distrust yourself."[2]

The Stoics thought they had a solution for this predicament. If we are to have a good life, we need to live in accordance with the proper values. At the same time, though, we need to take steps to inure ourselves to the insults that doing this will likely trigger. Let us now take a closer look at how the Stoics thought we could accomplish this.

IF SOMEONE HURTS US by insulting us, say the Stoics, we have only ourselves to blame. If we have chosen the proper values, an insult can do us no real harm—it cannot, that is, deprive us of anything that is genuinely valuable. (It can deprive us, of course, of social status, but as we have seen, the Stoics don't think this is valuable.) According to the Stoic philosopher Musonius Rufus, "those who do not know what is really good and what is really shameful, and who are overly concerned with their own fame—these people think that they are being injured if someone glares at them, laughs at them, hits them, or mocks them. But a man who is thoughtful and sensible—as a philosopher should be—is disturbed by none of these things. He believes that the shame comes not in being insulted but in behaving in an insulting manner."[3]

An insult can cause us pain, say the Stoics, only if we believe it has harmed us: "Remember," says Epictetus, "that what is insulting is not the person who abuses you or hits you, but the judgment about them that they *are* insulting."[4] He adds that "another person will not do you harm unless you wish it; you will be harmed at just that time at which you take yourself to be harmed."[5] But if we choose the proper values, an insult cannot do us any real harm. In particular, an insult cannot turn a person who is good, in the Stoic sense of the word, into a person who is bad. Keeping this in mind, the Stoics think, can deprive insults of their sting.

More generally, the Stoics think we are foolish to spend our days, as many people do, trying to control things over which we have little or no control. Do this, and we are bound to become deeply frustrated. One of the things over which we have little control, though, is what other people think of us. Even if we are extraordinarily nice to them—even if we give them a job, money for a car, and one of our kidneys—they might despise us. Consequently, if we spend our days trying to make others admire us, we are likely to experience considerable anxiety and little happiness.

We would do well, say the Stoics, to take the time and energy we might have spent seeking social status and instead spend it on something over which we have considerable control—namely, on choosing the correct values and living in accordance with them. We may not have it in our power to become someone who is loved and admired by all, but we do have it in our power to develop certain exemplary character traits—to become, for example, magnanimous, temperate, just, and courageous. As Marcus Aurelius—who, besides being a Stoic philosopher, happened to be a Roman emperor—reminds us, even though we don't have it in our power to stop others from sneering at us, we do have it in our power to do nothing that deserves a sneer.[6]

To better understand the Stoics' value system, consider the following question: would you rather have people think you are a good person when in fact you are a bad person, or think you are a bad person when in fact you are a good person? If you choose the first alternative—as I suspect most people will, albeit after some hemming and hawing—it is dramatic evidence of the extent to which you value fame. The Stoics, however, will unhesitatingly favor the second alternative: it is far better, they will insist, to be a good person and have people think you are bad than to be a bad person and have people think you are good. They would add that if you are a bad person, you are likely to have a bad life, no matter how highly others think of you, and that if you are a good person, you are likely to have a good life, no matter how poorly others think of you.

IF WE OVERCOME our craving for social status—if we stop playing what I shall call the *social hierarchy game*—we will find ourselves inhabiting a different world, socially speaking, than we formerly did. In particular, when someone insults us, it won't ruin our day the way it used to. Instead, we will calmly assess the event. We will realize that the insulter, because he values fame, is playing the social hierarchy game—he wants, that is, to maintain or improve his position on the social hierarchy. Furthermore, he assumes that we are playing this game as well; nearly everyone, after all, plays it. His insult, we will conclude, is a move in that game: he is trying to improve his standing on the social hierarchy, improve it at our expense. Since we no longer play the social hierarchy game, though, our "losing" this encounter won't matter to us.

To better understand this point, consider the following analogy. Suppose that as you are sitting in a park, someone comes up, taps you on the shoulder, shouts out "You're it!", and runs off. The person is obviously playing tag. How you respond to him depends on whether you are also playing the game. If you are, his touching you might upset you: in tag, after all, it is a bad thing to be "it." If, however, you are not playing the game, it is unlikely that this incident will upset you. Being touched, after all, did you no real harm. Furthermore, the person who touched you wasn't really trying to harm you; he was instead trying to win the game that he happens to be playing. On realizing this, you might respond to the incident with no response at all: you might continue sitting there as if nothing had happened. And if you do respond, it might be with an explanation: you might point out that you aren't a participant in the game he is playing.

If you tell someone you are a nonparticipant in the game of tag, he will likely respond by not tagging you again in the future: tagging you, after all, will be a waste of his tag-playing time. Similarly, if you make it clear to someone, by your indifference to her insults, that you are a noncombatant in the battle for social status, she might become less likely to tag you with insults in the future. Her insults, she will realize, are wasted on you. She might instead save them for her social rivals.

Something else might happen, though, when she discovers that you aren't playing the social hierarchy game: she might attempt to befriend you. It is, after all, difficult to befriend someone who insults you or who clearly thinks of himself as socially superior to you. If you withdraw from the social hierarchy game, though, you will suppress both your insulting tendencies and your self-promotional tendencies. People will therefore come to regard you as "socially safe"—as an individual, that is, against whom they don't have to compete in the battle for position on the social hierarchy. Such social noncombatants will presumably be easier to talk to, easier to confide in, and even easier to befriend than an ardent social gamer would.

I should add that the ancient Stoics seem to have experienced this phenomenon. Many of those who encountered the Stoics found them to be both impressive and likeable individuals. Zeno of Citium, the founder of Stoicism, was held in high enough esteem by his fellow Athenians that they gave him the keys to the city and honored him with a golden crown and bronze statue.[7] Seneca appears to have had no shortage of friends, and Musonius Rufus had friends who were devoted enough to follow him into exile on a desolate island.[8] Furthermore, the Stoic philosopher Euphrates of Tyre seems to have won the unabashed admiration of Pliny the Younger, who describes him as being "easy of access, unreserved, and actuated by those social principles he professes to teach." Pliny also comments on "the courtesy and engaging sweetness" of Euphrates's manner. He complains that his duties prevent him from conversing with Euphrates as much as he would like.[9]

But having said all this, I should add that there are individuals who, when they discover that someone is a noncombatant in the battle for social status, will not respond by leaving her alone or by appreciating her guileless conversation. To the contrary, they will continue to pummel her with insults; indeed, they might even start using her as a verbal punching bag on which they can practice their insult skills without fear of retaliation. Under these circumstances, the pacifist is well advised simply to sit back and watch the show. It might be useful for her to remind herself that in most cases, these individuals simply cannot help themselves. Because the social hierarchy game is so deeply ingrained in them, they have a hard time imagining that an interaction between humans can involve anything other than an exchange of insults. The habitual insulter, rather than provoking our anger, should provoke our pity.

WHAT DID THE STOICS VALUE, if not social status and affluence? One thing they valued was virtue. They thought, in other words, that we should strive to embody the ancient virtues: we should be courageous, magnanimous, just, self-disciplined, and so forth. Another thing they valued was tranquility. The tranquility sought by the Stoics, I should point out, was not the kind of tranquility one might attain by, say, downing a third martini. It was instead a state in which one is relatively free of negative emotions such as anger, fear, and grief, but filled with positive emotions, especially feelings of joy. The Stoics thought our chances of having a good and meaningful life were far greater if we pursued virtue and tranquility than if we pursued, as most people do, social status and affluence.

What, readers will naturally wonder, is wrong with pursuing social status and affluence? The problem is that we humans are evolutionarily programmed to be insatiable: our evolutionary ancestors who always craved more food, better housing, and a higher position on the social hierarchy were more likely to survive and reproduce than those who were easily satisfied in these matters. This means that if we pursue social status and affluence, we will go through life dissatisfied with what we have. We will continually believe that if only we had more—a bit more social status, a bit bigger house—we would live happily ever after. We will therefore work hard, or at least scheme extensively, to get that bit more. If we fail to get it, we will feel frustrated; if we succeed in getting it, we will soon take our gains for granted and will again feel frustrated.

In conclusion, if we seek social status and affluence, we are likely to go through life dissatisfied when we have it in our power to gain satisfaction: all we need to do is adopt the proper values—we need only, that is, pursue virtue and tranquility instead of fame and fortune. Many, I realize, will challenge this assertion. They will argue that those who attain fame and fortune do indeed live happily ever after—not always, maybe, but often. They will also point out that those who believe otherwise are in a very small minority.

I will not attempt here to defend the claim that we are better off pursuing tranquility than fame and fortune, inasmuch as I have defended it at length elsewhere.[10] I will take this opportunity, however, to point out that even though it is true that those who advocate pursuing tranquility rather than fame and fortune have always been in the minority, they are a rather impressive group of individuals. Among them we find not only the Stoic philosophers but such diverse thinkers as Arthur Schopenhauer, Henry David Thoreau, Buddha, Lao Tzu, and St. John of the Cross. One of the things these individuals have in common is that unlike most people, they thought very carefully about happiness and all the mistakes people make in their pursuit of it. We would perhaps do well to heed their advice on how best to live.

It should now be clear why the Stoics spent so much time thinking about insults. They sought tranquility. They therefore spent time devising strategies for dealing with tranquility-disrupting events. And because they realized that the insults of others are some of the most common and significant irritants of daily living, it was only natural for them to develop a strategy for preventing insults from upsetting them.

The Stoics ended up with a two-pronged strategy for dealing with insults. The first prong was concerned with their external response to insults. The Stoics were advocates, as we have seen, of insult pacifism. They thought that pacifism was likely to reduce the number of insults to which we would be subjected. The second prong of the Stoics' strategy was concerned with their internal response to insults. They believed that by choosing the proper values—in particular, by ceasing to value social status—we could prevent insults from upsetting us. As Musonius Rufus points out, a good person, when insulted, "will calmly and quietly bear what has happened, since this is appropriate behavior for a person who wants to be magnanimous."[11] Someone who employed both parts of their strategy, the Stoics maintained, not only would look calm in the face of insults but would actually be calm. He would, in other words, gain an immunity to insults.

It is worth noting that the two prongs of the Stoics' insult-response strategy are mutually reinforcing. To begin with, if we can remain internally calm in the face of insults, it will be relatively easy for us to respond, externally, to them as if nothing had happened: for us, nothing *will* have happened. Furthermore, by acting, externally, as if an insult is insignificant, we can reduce its internal significance to us. In particular, if we use self-deprecating humor in response to an insult, we put that insult into its proper place in the cosmic scheme of things: life is simply too short for us to spend it fretting over other people's petty jabs. On doing this, we will probably find it easier to "take" the insult. More generally, if we take ourselves too seriously, we are likely to be miserable; if, however, we learn to laugh at ourselves—which is what we are doing when we engage in self-deprecating humor—our days are likely to be much less stressful.

THE STOICS, AS WE HAVE SEEN, think that if we stop playing the social hierarchy game, we can become immune to insults. Significantly, they think we should take steps to become immune to praise as well. A Stoic will realize, after all, that people are most likely to praise us when we have done something that, according to their values, is a good thing to do. Thus, someone who values expensive watches might praise us for buying an expensive watch. (He might also, I should add, insult us for buying a $20 plastic watch that, as it so happens, keeps time as well as his $20,000 gold watch does.) But if someone's values are mistaken, his praise is likely to be misguided. It would therefore be inconsistent of us, once we have stopped playing the social hierarchy game, to shrug off other people's insults of us but not their praise.

Turning to the Stoics, we find that they indeed recommend that we internally dismiss other people's praise: at one point, for example, the Stoic philosopher Epictetus instructs us to respond to praise by laughing (to ourselves) at the person who praised us.[12] The Stoics had little to say, though, about what our external response should be. Under these circumstances, we might suspect that the Stoics' advice on the proper external response to praise would mirror their advice on how we should respond to insults. We might suspect, in other words, that they would advocate pacifism in response to both insults and praise. But what would this *praise pacifism* look like?

In the same way as an insult pacifist would ignore an insult—would carry on as if nothing had been said—a praise pacifist might say nothing in response to praise. Under some circumstances, I think this is a very effective response. Suppose, in particular, we think someone's praise of us is insincere. By carrying on as if nothing had been said, we not only discourage further praise, but let the flatterer know that we are on to him.

Under other circumstances, though, it is probably inadvisable to remain silent in response to praise. Suppose, for example, we think someone's praise of us is sincere (although perhaps misguided). If we remain silent, the person who praised us is likely to interpret our silence as a social put-down: our silence suggests that we *expect* him to praise us, which in turn suggests that we think he is below us on the social hierarchy. The Stoics, I suspect, would have been reluctant to inflict this sort of implied insult. They would instead have advocated doing *something* in response to sincere praise. The something in question presumably would have been minimal: we might, for example, respond to praise with a simple (but quite possibly insincere) "Thanks." And after saying it, we should carry on as if nothing had been said.

The Stoics would also, I think, have advocated self-deprecation in response to praise. If, for example, someone praises us for being awarded some honor, we might respond by denigrating ourselves: we might, for example, say, "You are very kind," the implication being that we didn't really deserve the honor. Alternatively, we can attribute our success to luck. Those around us will probably find this to be a satisfying response; indeed, when we fail to attribute an accomplishment to luck, they might be happy to do so on our behalf.

LET US PAUSE HERE to take a closer look at honors. Those who play the social hierarchy game are happy to receive honors; indeed, they will go to great lengths to gain them. According to historian Paul Johnson, for example, British politician and writer Roy Jenkins "collected baubles, such as peerages and honorific posts...with such immense enthusiasm and diplomatic skill" that he ended up with an astonishing number of honorary degrees—indeed, more than any other human being has collected.[13]

It can be awkward for someone who has abandoned the social hierarchy game to be awarded an honor. In particular, a Stoic will seek not *honors* but *honor*: he will, that is, strive to be an honorable individual, but it will be of little concern to him whether the world recognizes that he is an honorable individual and of less concern still whether they choose to recognize his honorableness in a public manner. Stated differently, a Stoic will do things because they are worth doing, not because he might be honored, or even admired, for doing them. What should a Stoic do, then, if despite not seeking it, an honor comes his way? Should he refuse it?

Probably not. Doing this would likely, as we saw back in chapter 4, insult those who bestowed the honor: "He thinks our honors are beneath him!" Furthermore, the public in general would likely regard the refusal as a churlish act. His best response, I think, is to graciously accept the honor and then be careful not to let it go to his head.

Having said this, I should add that from the mere fact that someone rejects honors, it does not follow that he is doing so because he has overcome his craving for social status. Indeed, declining honors can be an excellent way to improve one's position on the social hierarchy. Poet A. E. Housman, for example, made a point of declining all the honors that were offered to him, including six honorary degrees from British universities and the Order of Merit. On declining this last honor, though, he remarked on what a great distinction it was to have refused an OM.[14]

THE STOICS, AS WE HAVE SEEN, don't have a lot to say about what we should do in response to praise directed our way. Nor do they appear to be particularly forthcoming in their advice regarding the praise we might confer on someone else. At one point, Epictetus tells us that as we make progress as Stoics, we will stop praising others.[15] It seems unlikely, though, that the Stoics were completely averse to offering praise. One imagines, in particular, that the teachers of the Stoic schools would periodically have praised students for making progress in their study of Stoicism. One also imagines that the Stoics would have been willing to use praise to influence the behavior of the non-Stoics around them. Allow me to explain.

In my investigation of praise, I discovered that we inhabit a world in which people are reluctant to praise others and in which the praise they do offer is likely to be insincere. Why are we so stingy with praise? Because to praise someone sincerely, we have to admit to ourselves that he is worthy of praise, meaning, quite possibly, that he is in some respect better than we are. For lots of people, making such an admission to themselves is painful, and making such an admission in public is more painful still. Indeed, anyone playing the social hierarchy game will conclude that it is bad strategy to go around praising others. Doing so not only hurts your chances of rising on the social hierarchy, but improves their chances. In other words, praising other people is to the social hierarchy game as scoring an "own goal" is to soccer.

As a rule, we like to wait until people are dead before we publicly praise them. At their funeral, we present eulogies to them and go around telling everyone what wonderful people they used to be. By this time, of course, the person we are praising is out of earshot, and the praise can therefore do him no good. Why save our *eu logia*—our good words—for the dead and thereby waste them? Why not instead offer eulogies to the living? Because our obsession with our position on the social hierarchy prevents us from doing so.

Because praise is so rare in our culture—not rare from teachers to students or parents to children, perhaps, but rare from adults to adults—it can be a potent tool in our dealings with others. Furthermore, realize that for someone not playing the social hierarchy game, there are no costs associated with offering praise to others: he won't have to worry about the impact that offering praise will have on his social status. Such a person is therefore able to give away "for free" something that others value highly. In other words, someone who has taken Stoic advice to heart has little to lose and much to gain by using praise to encourage others.

Having said this, I should emphasize that the Stoics would not have advocated that we be indiscriminate in our praise, as proponents of the self-esteem movement (see chapter 7) are wont to do. For the Stoics, the point of praising someone is not to boost his self-esteem but to help him become a better person—become, that is, a more virtuous person in the ancient sense of the word. Become virtuous, the Stoics would have argued, and you will experience self-esteem, regardless of what others think of you.

ONE THING I DISCOVERED in my investigation of praise is that praising others can have untoward consequences. Most of the people we praise, after all, will still be playing the social hierarchy game. Consequently, if we praise them, it is possible that they will construe our praise as a sign of social submission—as a sign, that is, that we are conceding defeat to them in the battle for position on the social hierarchy. As a result, they might start looking down on us. They might even start behaving haughtily toward us, in which case our praise will lose its impact.

More generally, praising someone can undermine our relationship with him. Consider, for example, a young woman's relationship with her boyfriend. If she constantly praises him and tells him how wonderful he is, there is a danger that he will start taking her for granted. He might even regard her as being a sure thing, as far as dating is concerned, and might therefore set about finding someone better. To avoid this fate, the young woman might play hard to get. She might, that is, not only withhold praise but go out of her way to create the impression that she doesn't think the boyfriend is particularly wonderful.

It is also possible for our praise to embarrass its recipient, particularly if the praise is offered in public. This behavior, to be sure, is paradoxical, particularly in a society in which people are, as I've said, starved for praise. I think what people fear is that too much praise will make them the target of other people's ridicule or, even worse, their envy. Thus, public praise, if too lavish, can jeopardize the recipient's social standing rather than enhance it.

In my investigation of praise, I explored ways to praise people without incurring these and other side effects. One of the techniques I uncovered involves mixing praise with insults. Along these lines, when mathematician G. H. Hardy wanted to praise someone, he prefaced the praise with a slightly derogatory remark.[16] Why do such a thing? Because it makes public praise more palatable.

Not only that, but by prefacing praise with an insult, we enhance the subsequent praise. In chapter 4, we examined ambush insults in which someone offers false praise as a setup for an insult: by prefacing the insult with praise, we make the emotional impact of the insult that much greater. What Hardy did is the reverse of an ambush insult—call it *ambush praise*. The praised person will be bracing himself to hear more insults and will therefore be delighted when the initial insult is instead followed by praise. Notice, too, that by mixing insult with praise we can make our praise more credible: flatterers, after all, are unlikely to punctuate their praise with insults.

During my investigation of praise, I also witnessed several incidents in which people, instead of putting insults before words of praise, followed words of praise with insults. This sounds, I realize, like an ambush insult, but there is an important difference. Consider again the case we examined back in chapter 4, in which a relative responded to a businessman's success by telling him that "You've gone far in life . . . for someone who never even finished high school." This could have been meant as an ambush insult, but not necessarily. It is also possible that the relative, when he started talking, sincerely intended to praise the businessman, but that as soon as the words of praise were out of his mouth, he started worrying that they would be taken as an admission of social inferiority. Therefore, perhaps without even realizing what he was doing, he followed the praise with a subtle put-down.

In chapter 2, we explored backbiting—saying insulting things about someone to someone else. We considered a hypothetical case in which Alice told Betty insulting things about Carol. In my research on praise, I explored the praise equivalent of backbiting—call it *backrubbing*. To backrub is to praise someone to someone else: thus, instead of insulting Carol to Betty, Alice might tell Betty what a wonderful person Carol is. In the same way as backbiting comments can get back to the person whose back was bit, backrubbing comments can get back to the person who was praised. If this person is playing the social hierarchy game, she will probably be quite delighted that you are going around telling people nice things about her. This means that backrubbing is a wonderful way to praise someone. In particular, it avoids the negative side effects that can arise when we praise her to her face.

By engaging in backrubbing, by the way, Alice can influence the behavior not only of Carol but of Betty as well. In particular, Betty might start doing the things Alice is praising Carol for doing, in the belief that doing so will gain her Alice's admiration and might even cause Alice to praise *her* behind her back.

The Stoics were quite interested in helping the people around them have better lives. They don't specifically mention the above backrubbing technique, but I think it would serve their purposes nicely. As we have seen, they place little value on social status. This means that they can praise others "for free"; if doing so causes them to lose social status, big deal! The people who receive their praise, though, will likely place a high value on it. Carefully chosen words of praise, delivered in the right way, can therefore play an important role in motivating other people to change the way they live their lives.

IN CHAPTER 9, WE SAW THAT one way to respond to an insult is by behaving dismissively toward it or toward the person who unleashed it. It should by now be clear that Stoics will dismiss both insults and insulters. If you insult a Stoic, he will conclude that you are doing so because you have adopted mistaken personal values—adopted them for the simple reason that you have never taken the time to reflect carefully about what in life is worth possessing.

It is important to realize, however, that even though Stoics will dismiss those who insult them, they won't offer the kinds of openly dismissive responses we explored in chapter 9. They won't, in particular, respond to an insult by saying, "What makes you think I care what you think about me?" They won't say this even though they in fact *don't* care what you, with your mistaken values, think about them.

It is also important to realize that Stoics won't refuse to have dealings with the people they dismiss. Stoics believe they have a duty to serve their fellow man, and they realize that to fulfill this duty, they will routinely have to have dealings with people whose values are mistaken and who, as a result, are likely to insult them. This realization was one of the things that motivated the Stoics to develop strategies to prevent insults from upsetting them. By employing these strategies, they could minimize the unpleasantness of their dealings with insulting individuals.

Although the Stoics did not refuse to have dealings with individuals whose values were mistaken, they did not seek their company either. In particular, the Stoics thought that when we choose our friends, we should be careful to choose people with correct values. If, after all, we spend our time associating with people with mistaken values, there is a very real danger that their values will contaminate ours: as Epictetus puts it, "if a person's companion is dirty the person who spends time with him, even if he happens to be clean, is bound to become dirty too."[17]

FROM THE FACT THAT Stoics will shrug off the criticisms and praise of those whose values are mistaken, it does not follow that they will shrug off *all* insults and praise. In particular, if they think someone's values are correct, they will take that person's criticisms and praise to heart. Thus, in the ancient world, a pupil in a Stoic school of philosophy would have cared very much what his teacher thought of him.

Another thing to realize is that although the Stoics will reflexively shrug off the insults inflicted on them by people with mistaken values, they will, in the act of shrugging, pause momentarily to consider whether there might be a grain of truth in the insult. Metaphorically speaking, they will pause to see whether the rock that has been thrown at them is a diamond. To understand this behavior, we need to keep in mind that the Stoics regarded themselves as works in progress: they thought that one of the most important undertakings in life is an unending program of self-improvement. The Stoics realized that we tend to be blind to our own shortcomings and as a result that other people often have greater insight into our motivations than we do. This means that it is possible for us to use the insults others inflict on us as a tool for self-discovery.

But what if someone's remarks about us are obviously motivated by malice? What if she has declared herself to be our enemy? Even under these circumstances, the Stoic will pause, in the process of dismissing his enemy's insults, to search them for grains of truth. The Stoics were, after all, intellectual descendants of the Cynics, and it was the Cynic philosopher Antisthenes who recommended that we pay attention to our enemies, inasmuch as they will usually be the first to discover our mistakes.[18] By way of contrast, our friends tend to look for what is good about us and tell us things we want to hear. Thus, the comments of our enemies, though no fun to hear, can be rather more useful to us than the comments of our friends—if, at any rate, our goal is self-improvement. Our friends will help us hide from ourselves; our enemies won't.

Suppose that after inspecting an insult, a Stoic finds that it contains nothing he can use in his program of self-development. To the contrary, the only thing the insult reveals is just how bad a person the insulter is. On being the target of such insults, a Stoic won't get mad and seek vengeance by inflicting counterinsults; he will instead remember the observation of Marcus Aurelius that the best way to take revenge on a bad person is to refuse to be like him.[19] Indeed, the Stoic might even find it reassuring that a bad person would insult him. What would be disturbing is if the bad person complimented him on how he was living his life!

More generally, as part of their self-improvement program, Stoics seek out role models, individuals they think are better than themselves and from whom they can therefore learn to become better people. Stoics will also realize that even though another person is flawed in many respects, he might have profound insights into one aspect of life, and they will be happy to use this individual as a limited role model: they will learn what they can from him about his area of expertise.

When a chosen role model criticizes a Stoic, he will not take the criticism as an insult and therefore will not respond by getting angry. Or if he does experience anger, it will be directed not at the mentor but at himself: he will be angry for being so slow to overcome the flaw his mentor criticized. Indeed, when his mentor makes a critical remark, the Stoic will realize that it is in a sense a compliment: the fact that the mentor would take the time to criticize him is, after all, evidence that the mentor does not take him to be a hopeless case. He might therefore respond to the criticism with sincere thanks.

The behavior of Stoics, by the way, is likely to puzzle modern psychologists. Stoics don't fight back when insulted, they are critical of themselves, and they are indifferent to praise. Such behavior is usually a symptom of low self-esteem and possibly even depression, but the Stoics appear to be both self-confident and cheerful. How can this be?

To understand Stoic behavior, it is important to realize that Stoics do something that most people refuse to do—namely, take personal responsibility for their happiness. Thus, if they are unhappy, Stoics don't reflexively blame the world; instead, they set about reexamining their values to see if these values are mistaken. Additionally, they might investigate whether there is a better strategy they can use in their response to external events, a strategy that will prevent these events from having a negative impact on their happiness. And after doing these things, they are unlikely to feel it necessary to make an appointment with a psychologist.

THIS, THEN, IS THE STOIC STRATEGY for dealing with insults. As far as our external response is concerned, they advocate insult pacifism, and as far as our internal response is concerned, they advocate a fairly radical self-transformation. To achieve the transformation in question, we must reexamine our values and thereafter work to overcome our craving for social status, and along with it, our craving for material affluence. Many readers, I think, will be willing to experiment with insult pacifism; far fewer, I suspect, will be willing to undergo the personal transformation I have described.

I sympathize with these readers. Undertaking a Stoic-inspired program of self-improvement will, after all, be a humbling experience. Most of us go through life thinking we are pretty much perfect: we like ourselves just the way we are. If we follow Stoic advice, though, we will have to learn to think of ourselves, as Epictetus puts it, as an enemy lying in wait.[20] We will not only have to admit that we are flawed, but spend time and energy identifying each individual flaw so we can correct it. This sounds like no fun at all.

Undertaking a program of self-improvement will also be emotionally unsatisfying. When, for example, an enemy insults us, we won't be able to hurl back a counterinsult; we will instead have to carefully consider whether his insult contains a grain of truth. And finally, undertaking a program of self-improvement will typically mean granting other people "mentor status." Because we have grown up playing the social hierarchy game, though, we will find it hard to admit that we have anything important to learn from others.

It is understandable that people would be reluctant to embark on the program of personal transformation advocated by the Stoics. If they have an "insult problem," they will instead focus their attention on the insults that are giving them trouble. But if the Stoics are right, the pain caused by these insults is merely a symptom of a much more deeply rooted and much more serious malady—namely, living in accordance with the wrong values. According to the Stoics, until we deal with this malady, we will experience, besides pain on being insulted, many other negative emotions, including anger, anxiety, grief, and envy.

Those wishing to have a good life, then, would be well advised, when determining how best to deal with insults, to consider the possibility that the Stoics were onto something—that perhaps the time has come to take a long, hard look at the values by which they live.

CHAPTER 12

Insights

IN CONJUNCTION WITH MY RESEARCH for this book and more generally, as a result of studying the Stoic philosophers, I have, in recent years, undertaken an experiment: I have tried to live in accordance with Stoic advice regarding insults. This has meant practicing pacifism with respect to insults: I have tried to train myself not to inflict first-strike insults, not to backbite, and not to respond to insults with malicious insults. More significantly, it has meant working on my "inner insult game": I have tried to transform myself so that my internal response to insults matches my external response. My goal, in other words, is not merely to look calm in the face of insults but actually to remain calm. To achieve the transformation in question, I have reassessed my values in accordance with Stoic advice, and as a result of this reassessment, I have attempted to withdraw from the social hierarchy game. In this closing chapter, I would like to report on the outcome of this experiment.

LET ME BEGIN by describing my experience with insult pacifism. The Stoic strategy of not responding to an insult is, I have found, quite effective. Indeed, it is likely that the more severe the insult, the more reason there is to respond to it with no response at all. Allow me to explain.

Recently, I was driving down the road, and because traffic was heavy, I was having trouble moving out of the left lane to clear the way for faster vehicles. A motorcycle wove through traffic until it came up behind me. It tailgated me for a while and then finally zipped around me on the right. At the next traffic light, the motorcycle was just ahead of me. The rider turned around and flipped me the bird. I did not react to his insult but merely looked at him, impassively. He must have assumed that I did not see his gesture, because he flipped me the bird again, this time with vigor. I remained impassive. He turned his back on me and sped off into the distance as soon as the light changed.

Not responding to his insult was, I am convinced, the best possible response. By behaving pacifistically in these circumstances, I accomplished two things: I seem to have frustrated the insulter, and far more significantly, I prevented myself from getting upset over an insult that might otherwise have ruined my day.

On another occasion, I was the target of severe verbal abuse in a public setting. The incident took place while I was out rowing a racing shell. Unlike rowing a rowboat, a canoe, or even a kayak, rowing a racing shell is a hazardous activity. The boats in question are built for speed, not stability, and as a result, they are quite tippy. They want to be upside down, and it is only through skillful use of his oars that a rower can prevent this from happening. Indeed, let go of an oar for even a split second, and he will likely find himself under water.

When I was learning to row, I flipped boats on two occasions, but then I went through a long (literally) dry spell and, predictably, started thinking I was unflippable. Thanks in part to my overconfidence, I was out rowing one day when my right oar hit an obstacle in the water. I'm not sure what happened, but I do know that a moment later, I found myself looking up through blue-green water at a very distant sun. I popped back to the surface, and started swimming my boat toward the riverbank so I could get back in.

It was then that I became aware of laughter. An interstate highway passes over the river near where I was rowing. Traffic was stalled, and a trucker had been watching me row. Much to his surprise (and mine), I had flipped my boat. He found this to be quite amusing. He also took it as an opportunity to tell me, in great detail and with some verbal ingenuity, just how little he thought of me. He started shouting how dumb I am, how foolish I look, what an ass I am, and how I probably won't be able to get back in the boat. In between these comments, he engaged in raucous laughter. I ignored the truck driver and concentrated instead on getting back into my boat. I assumed that he would quickly tire of insulting me, but because of the stalled traffic, he apparently had nothing else to do, meaning that the insults just kept coming. If there were a Richter scale for insults, this would have been an 8.0.

After maybe two minutes of his shouts and laughter, I felt anger rising within me and considered flashing him a gesture that would indicate what I thought of him. But since his goal in insulting me was to upset me, I reasoned that by making such a gesture, I would only be providing him with evidence that he had accomplished his goal. He would, if anything, laugh louder. So I continued my nonresponse. The traffic finally started to move again, and his laughter receded into the distance. I managed to get back into my boat and started rowing back to the dock, drenched and a bit flustered.

As I rowed, I reflected on the incident. Had I vented my anger at the truck driver, I thought, it probably would not have lessened that anger in the way that venting steam from a boiler lessens the boiler pressure. Indeed, anger seems to be a self-fueling emotion: to vent it is to feed it. Nor, I thought, would expressing my anger have made me feel better in the long run. For one thing, had I expressed my anger, I would now have felt disappointed with myself. Furthermore, expressing my anger probably would have increased the chance that I would feel angry about the incident in the future—that I would experience, that is, anger flashbacks (which are the insult equivalent of posttraumatic stress disorder). My pacifism in the face of the truck driver's insults, I concluded, might not have been emotionally satisfying, but it was, all things considered, the best way to have responded.

I was also convinced that by not venting my anger, I inflicted more harm on my insulter than any other response would have. I may have looked foolish down in the river in a capsized boat, but he must have looked more foolish still in his failed attempt to provoke me. He must have felt singularly impotent: "These are great insults, and yet they are having no apparent effect on this guy! None at all! What gives?" He was persistent in his insults, I think, for the simple reason that he needed, fairly desperately, to salvage the situation. He was like someone who, after making an unsound investment, starts throwing good money after bad, in an attempt to show some return for his efforts and thereby save face.

The man who had insulted me, I concluded, deserved not my anger but my pity. What sort of person, after all, would abuse a complete stranger the way he did—indeed, would abuse someone who, having just flipped a boat, was in a degree of physical danger? This person, I thought, must have learned this behavior somewhere. Presumably, he himself had been the target of similar insults in the past, and rather than trying to achieve a self-transformation that would immunize him against such insults, he had allowed the insults to transform him into a hateful individual—the human equivalent of a barking dog.

By the time I arrived at the dock, I felt, more than anything, amused and enlightened by the episode. This itself came as a bit of a surprise. There was a time, after all, when insults were capable of causing me pain but little else. My attitude toward insults had clearly changed. Indeed, after having spent a few years thinking, reading, and writing about insults, I found myself looking forward to being insulted. It gave me, after all, an opportunity to practice my insult pacifism. I also found that I had, over the years, become something of an insult connoisseur. Viewed in this context, the truck driver had presented me with a real gift: "This insult," I told myself, "is going into the book. I wish I knew who he was so I could send a thank-you note."

Although I have had good luck with nonresponse as my strategy for dealing with insults, my standard strategy—particularly when the insulter, unlike the one just described, is close enough to talk to—is to respond with self-deprecating humor. It is a response, I have found, that comes naturally for me; there is, after all, so much about me that I find laughable. I have, in my practice of insult pacifism, reached a stage at which, when people insult me, I almost reflexively attempt to top their insult: "Let me assure you, it's even worse than you suggest!"

Using self-deprecating humor, I have found, is also a wonderful anger-prevention technique. In the moments just after someone has insulted me, my attention is focused not on assessing the degree to which the insult has damaged my social standing but instead on how I can turn the insult into a joke. Distracting myself in this manner seems to prevent anger from taking root within me.

I have also experimented with a radical form of self-deprecation. A Stoic will, of course, apologize if in a moment of weakness he insults someone (in a malicious rather than playful manner). I have experimented, though, with apologizing when *someone insults me.* And by this, I don't mean apologizing in the insincere manner described in chapter 9—saying, "You have insulted me, but not to worry: all is forgiven." I instead mean sincerely taking responsibility for someone's having insulted me. Allow me to explain.

On one occasion, when someone expressed regret for having insulted me, I responded as follows: "It is perfectly understandable that you would say what you did. I'm a provocative person, and I bring out this sort of thing in other people. Really, I'm to blame." And in saying this, I was being perfectly sincere. Part of my role as philosopher is to act as an intellectual irritant to those around me—to make them rethink the things they take for granted. Indeed, this is, I think, the most socially useful thing philosophers do. (There is, I should add, a difference between being socially useful and being socially popular; Socrates found this out the hard way.) Most people don't want to rethink their beliefs, though, and they therefore respond to philosophical provocations with insults.

On another occasion, I found myself at a meeting during which I was invited to give my opinion on a certain sensitive matter. I did so, only to discover that other people not only rejected my opinion but felt compelled to attack me for having expressed it. Indeed, one person started telling me, with his voice raised and in some detail, what he thought of me. In response, I did not likewise engage in invective. (Or should I say that I don't *remember* engaging in invective; I would be the first to admit that in cases like this, our memories play tricks on us.) Instead, I held my tongue, and after the meeting was over, I went up to the person in private and told him that I wanted to apologize: "Things got pretty heated in there," I explained. I held out my hand. He shook it.

We live in a culture in which people, when they make a mistake, rarely apologize. Instead, they tend to blame something—or, better still, someone else—for the mistake. They know that admitting a mistake can damage the image of themselves that they are trying to project, which in turn can damage their social standing among their rivals in the social hierarchy game. If they can succeed in placing the blame for their mistake on someone else, however, they might damage that person's social standing and thereby improve their own standing relative to his. Thus, someone playing the social hierarchy game has lots of reasons for not apologizing.

If you have stopped playing this game, though, you will have overcome the principal impediment to apologetic behavior. It may be true that by apologizing, you lose points in the social hierarchy game, but to you these points are worthless, so you won't mind losing them. As a result, you will find it easy to apologize for your mistakes, something that previously would have been socially difficult for you to do. You might even find yourself, as I did, apologizing for the insults that others direct at you, an act which at one time would have been socially unthinkable.

LET US NOW TURN our attention from my behavior as a target of insults to my behavior as an insulter. Insult pacifists, as we have seen, will not respond to insults with malicious counterinsults. This means that my own practice of pacifism still needs work: I still, on occasion, respond to insults with sarcastically dismissive remarks. In my old prepacifist days, I had, I am told, a real talent for this sort of thing, and old habits die hard.

We have also seen that insult pacifists won't inflict first-strike insults. I don't think that even in my prepacifist days I was a particularly prolific source of first-strike insults—but again, our memory can deceive us about such things. One thing I will confess to is being a prolific source of "stealth insults." When, for example, I was driving my car and someone cut me off in traffic or was slow to start moving after a stoplight changed, I tended to get angry, and in my anger I might call him an idiot or even something worse. In retrospect, what I find interesting about these incidents is that I would heap invective on the other driver only when my windows, and preferably his as well, were rolled up, meaning that he couldn't hear what I said. It is now clear to me that such insults are a waste of time and energy. Yelling insults at someone who can't hear me accomplishes nothing but to disrupt my own tranquility. Since gaining this insight, I have made considerable progress in reducing the frequency with which I yell, stealthily, at other drivers.

I also used to engage in another, socially more significant form of insult, namely, backbiting: I would say insulting things to someone about a person who wasn't present. I would love to be able to say that as a result of my experiment in pacifism I have overcome backbiting, but I haven't. One thing that has changed, though, is that when I do backbite, I am far more likely to be aware of what I am doing than was formerly the case. When I catch myself backbiting, I feel annoyed at myself and ashamed of my behavior, and this, to be sure, has taken much of the fun out of backbiting.

I have, in recent years, come to appreciate just how fine the line is between talking about someone and talking someone down. I will find myself talking with a friend, relative, or colleague about some mutual acquaintance. We might be discussing some problem this acquaintance is having, trying to decide what, if anything, we can do to help him. All too often, I have discovered, these potentially beneficent conversations degenerate into backbiting: we start to discuss, with some glee, the shortcomings, mistakes, and failures of the acquaintance. But because our conversation started out with noble motives, we do not see our backbiting for what it is.

When speaking about someone else, it is very important, I have concluded, to monitor our emotions, inasmuch as these emotions will reveal to us our true motives in saying what we are saying. If we are talking about someone with the goal of helping him, we will discover the warm glow of sympathy within us. As long as that glow is present, we can safely continue our conversation. But in an instant, that glow can transform into a gleeful feeling that is simultaneously malicious and delicious—a feeling of delight that the person we are discussing is having the problems he is having. That is the sign that backbiting has begun, and if we are working to overcome our insulting tendencies, it is the moment at which we will stop talking.

ALTHOUGH I HAVE MADE some progress with the insults involved in backbiting, there is another sort of blatant insult that I continue to inflict without hesitation. The insults in question are those involved in playful teasing. These insults, as I have explained, help us form and maintain close relationships with other people. But in the same way as my experiment with pacifism has caused me to become more wary about what I say in conversations about people who aren't present, it has caused me to be more careful in my playful teasing. I have come to realize, in particular, that the insults inflicted in playful teasing aren't always as benign as one might think. They sometimes contain a malicious element, designed to put their target in his place, socially speaking. It is possible, in other words, for malicious insults to masquerade as playful teasing. On realizing this, I have become, I hope, kinder and gentler in my teasing.

My biggest discovery with respect to my behavior as an insulter was the realization that although I don't inflict lots of blatant, malicious insults, I am a prolific source of subtle insults. I started replaying conversations in my head in an attempt to figure out why I had said the things I did. On doing this, I became painfully aware of the extent to which, even in casual conversations, I am motivated by a desire to put the other person in his place, socially speaking—to demonstrate, in a subtle manner, the various respects in which he isn't better than I am.

I described one such case in chapter 1: in the process of congratulating a student for getting accepted to a graduate school, I subtly belittled the acceptance in question. Here is another example of this sort of thing. Suppose a colleague tells me how much trouble he has had getting a paper published. I might tell him to keep trying and, in passing, mention the papers I have recently had accepted for publication. There are two levels on which to understand my comments: either I am trying to cheer him up by showing him what is possible, or I am demonstrating to him that my work is more publishable than his, meaning that my work is superior to his, meaning (according to the curious logic of social hierarchies) that I am superior to him.

Along similar lines, suppose a friend describes his vacation to me. In response, I might describe my own, rather more luxurious vacation. Again, the conversation can be interpreted on two levels. To a disinterested outsider, it might sound like we are simply discussing vacations. At a deeper level, though, we are engaged in a bit of subtle social sparring: in comparing our vacations, we are, among other things, comparing our financial wherewithal, which in turn is connected to our social status.

I might be alone on the planet in doing this sort of thing, but I suspect not. What makes me different is not the rate at which I inflict subtle insults but the realization that I do it. When people engage in what looks like idle chitchat, it is often possible, if we listen carefully, to detect maneuvers in the social hierarchy game. In most cases, though, those who play this game aren't fully aware that this is what they are doing; indeed, if we accused them of doing it, they would probably resent the accusation. This only goes to show how deeply the social hierarchy game is embedded into our thought processes.

INASMUCH AS IT WAS MY GOAL to stop playing the social hierarchy game, I had to alter my behavior not only with respect to insults but with respect to praise. What I discovered, much to my surprise, was that it was easier for me to shrug off the insults directed at me than to shrug off the praise that came my way. Sad to say, I am a praise junkie. My external response to praise may have changed, but my internal response is approximately the same as it was before I started studying the Stoics: I experience this delightful rush, this happy little glow, when others say nice things about me. Not only that, but the source of the praise doesn't seem to matter: I am shamefully promiscuous with respect to praise.

And this is just one component of my praise problem. The Stoics, as we have seen, would tolerate our praising others under certain circumstances: by offering such praise, we can influence their behavior. The Stoics would be quite intolerant, though, of our praising ourselves. Indeed, according to Epictetus, one sign that I am making progress toward becoming a better person would be that I stop talking about myself as "a person who amounts to something or knows something."[1] I suspect that I have reduced the amount of outright boasting I do, but I remain a prolific source of a rather more subtle form of self-promotion.

Above, I gave examples of conversations in which I subtly insulted the person to whom I was talking. In these same conversations, though, we can find elements of self-promotion. I went out of my way in the first conversation to let a colleague know of my publication record and in the second conversation to let a friend know of my affluence. Here is another example of self-promotion that is simultaneously trivial and illuminating, drawn from a recent conversation. When someone thanked me for helping him with a math problem, I could simply have said "You are welcome," but instead of this Stoically proper response, I offered an explanation of my math ability: "One of my two undergraduate majors was math." In this simple statement, I multiply promoted myself: I informed the other person, by implication, that I am a college graduate, that as an undergraduate I had not one but two majors, and that I went on to graduate school.

In conjunction with my research on self-praise, I invented a zero-to-ten scale on which to rate people's self-promotional tendencies. Someone having a self-aggrandizement scale rating—let us call it a *SAS number*, for short—of zero would never praise herself. She might have won a gold medal in the

Olympics, but you would never know it from conversing with her. Indeed, if you learned of this accomplishment, you would have done so indirectly, perhaps by finding the medal buried in her sock drawer or by reading about it in her obituary. The Stoics, as far as I can tell, occupied this end of the self-aggrandizement scale.

Someone whose SAS number was ten, by way of contrast, would be a volcano of self-promotion. Start a conversation with this person about the high price of gasoline, and she would, within a matter of sentences, have turned the conversation into a vehicle for informing you what a wonderful person she is. When the conversation was over, you would walk away knowing, among other things, about the elite university she attended, about how much her engagement ring cost, and about how she was recently listed as one of the top pediatricians in the state. You would also have learned about her "problems": about how hard it is, anymore, to find tradespeople capable of installing slate roofs, about how expensive ski trips to St. Moritz have become, and about all the strings she had to pull to get Elvis Costello to perform at her recent birthday party, which was attended by more than a hundred of her closest friends.

After devising the self-aggrandizement scale, I wondered what my own SAS number would be. I imagined that others would rate me a four—at worst a five—and I did an experiment to check the accuracy of this self-assessment. I explained to my wife how the scale worked, and we had a discussion about where various people we knew would fall on the scale. I then suggested that I would rate, say, a six on the scale.

I expected her to try to talk me down—"No, honey, you're at worst a four"—but she said nothing in response. Somewhat baffled by her silence, I decided to do further research. The next day, I repeated the experiment on a close friend, only this time, after explaining the scale, I told him that I imagined I was a seven, instead of the six I had floated in the presence of my wife. He also said nothing in response.

The inescapable conclusion: in the eyes of those who know me best, my SAS number is *at least* an eight. Yikes! And I have this number despite being convinced that I reveal to others only a tiny fraction of the wonderful things about myself that I could reveal. Double yikes! I clearly have my work cut out for me, if my goal is to stop playing the social hierarchy game.

AFTER EXPERIENCING MY EPIPHANY regarding self-promotion, I undertook a program to reduce my SAS number. When I talked to others, I carefully monitored my conversation, trying to filter out self-promotional utterances. This, I quickly discovered, is hard to do. The problem is that the self-censorship in question must take place in real time. I tended to blurt out self-promotional sentences before I even knew what I was doing.

One way to reduce my conversational self-promotion, I decided, would be to place certain topics onto a mental do-not-mention list. Then I could simply avoid those topics in conversation. If, for example, I received some career-related good news, I would vow to myself to keep the news a secret. Such vows, I discovered, were remarkably ineffective. As soon as I encountered other people, I would find some way to wedge my news into the conversation. I discovered that I could no more hold in good news than I could, after sniffing a handful of pepper, hold in a sneeze.

Still anxious to reduce my SAS number, I turned my attention to my e-mails. It would be far easier, I reasoned, to deal with my self-promotional tendencies in e-mails than in conversations. You can't, after all, blurt something out in an e-mail; you always have the ability to reconsider what you have written before you hit the send button. And so I started checking my e-mails for elements of self-promotion. I was depressed to discover that many of my e-mails consisted almost exclusively of self-promotion, meaning that when I deleted the self-promotional content from an e-mail, what remained simply wasn't worth sending. My computer's trash bin started filling with aborted e-mails.

Another thing I discovered, while attempting to reduce my SAS number, is that if you refuse to self-promote, people can take it as a sign that you are keeping them at arm's length, socially speaking. (This is also, as we have seen, how they will respond if you discourage their playful teasing.) Alternatively, they might take it as a sign that you are in a grumpy mood: this, at any rate, was the diagnosis I got from a friend who attended a party with me at which, because I was avoiding self-promotion, I had little to say. I have concluded that people expect others to self-promote in conversations. And I suspect that it isn't just that they tolerate such behavior; they welcome it, inasmuch as it gives them an opportunity to reciprocally self-promote.

After making these discoveries, I decided that it was best to take the middle path with respect to self-promotion: I would self-promote some but not too much. I would also attempt to offset the self-praise I inflicted on others with a more than counterbalancing measure of self-deprecation.

THIS IS WHEN I had one final epiphany regarding self-promotion. One day, as I was congratulating myself on the progress I had made in reducing my SAS number (from an eight down to maybe a seven), it dawned on me that my avoidance of self-promotion, rather than being evidence that I was successfully abandoning the social hierarchy game, might in fact be evidence that I was playing that game more skillfully than ever. After all, the best way to win the admiration of others is not to beat them over the head with your accomplishments but to cleverly arrange things so that they discover your accomplishments on their own.

By way of illustration, a person who periodically reminds an acquaintance how it felt to stand on the medals podium of the Olympics will likely gain that acquaintance's admiration. The admiration in question, though, will be pale in comparison to the admiration the Olympian would (ultimately) gain if she never mentioned her victory but instead cleverly arranged for the acquaintance to "accidentally" come across an Olympic medal at the bottom of her sock drawer.

Is this what I am doing? Is my program to stop self-promoting really just a clever way to promote myself? Perhaps. Likewise, perhaps my dismissive attitude toward praise isn't the result of my deciding not to concern myself with what others think of me; perhaps it is simply a display of false modesty—indeed, modesty so false that I have succeeded in deceiving myself with it.

I finally came to realize that my battle to overcome the evolutionary programming that makes me care about social status will never be won. In retrospect, it was foolish for me to think that in part of one lifetime I could undo a few billion years of evolution. Indeed, I am as unlikely to overcome this programming as I am to overcome the evolutionary programming that makes ice cream taste so good and sprained ankles feel so bad. My goal, I concluded, should be not to extinguish my craving for social status but to suppress it to the extent that I can.

One imagines that overcoming the impulse to play the social hierarchy game is like overcoming an addiction to alcohol. To succeed we need, first of all, to admit that we have a problem. (This, I have done.) Then we need to work, in a very conscious manner, to deal with that problem. (This, I am doing.) After we have made progress, we should expect occasional relapses. And finally, it is unlikely that we will ever be completely "cured." Just as the recovering alcoholic will periodically discover in himself an impulse to drink, the recovering social-status addict will periodically hear a voice in his head that demands, when he has been insulted, that he strike back. This same voice will also, when someone tells him about her accomplishments, tell him to subtly downplay those accomplishments and to boast about his own, rather grander accomplishments. Perhaps the most he can hope for is to reduce this voice to a whisper.

Zeno, the original Stoic, claimed that the practice of Stoicism could affect a person's dreams.[2] When I first encountered this claim, I was puzzled by how such a thing could happen. Then, in conjunction with my program to curb my self-promotional tendencies, it happened. I had a dream in which I was going to meet a friend. I had just received some good news, and I thought about how fun it would be to share this news. But then my inner Stoic pointed out that my primary reason for sharing the news would be to make myself look good in the eyes of this friend. I decided it was best to keep the news to myself. I was self-censoring in a dream! A sign, perhaps, of progress?

Although I plan to continue my experiment in responding Stoically to insults and praise, I have learned the importance, as I do so, of keeping firmly in mind Stoic philosopher Seneca's comment regarding his own program of self-improvement: "Require not from me that I should be equal to the best, but that I should be better than the wicked. It is enough for me if every day I reduce the number of my vices, and blame my mistakes."[3]

Notes

One

1. Grothe, 4.
2. Kowalski, "Aversive Interpersonal Behaviors," 16.
3. Psalms 22: 6–7, New English Bible.
4. Proverbs 12:16, New English Bible.
5. Psalms 74: 18, New English Bible.
6. Jeremiah 3:6, New English Bible.
7. Cooley and Cooley, 77.
8. Seneca, "On Firmness," X.2.
9. Seneca, "On Anger," III.36–37.
10. *King Lear*, Act II, Scene 2.
11. Elizabethan Curse Generator website. http://trevorstone.org/curse/.
12. *Book of Classic Insults*, 40.
13. Price, 20.
14. *Book of Classic Insults*, 42.
15. Mencken, 140.
16. *Book of Insults, Ancient & Modern*, 121.
17. *Book of Insults, Ancient & Modern*, 123.
18. *Book of Classic Insults*, 149.
19. *Book of Classic Insults*, 153.
20. *Book of Insults, Ancient & Modern*, 134.
21. Grothe, 22.
22. The results of this research are reported in my *Guide to the Good Life*.

Two

1. *American Heritage Dictionary of the American Language*.
2. Tedeschi and Bond, 279.

3. Found in the online publication *Uncyclopedia*, under its entry for "ignorance." http://uncyclopedia.org/wiki/Ignorance.

4. Mathforum website. http://mathforum.org/kb/thread.jspa?forumID=13&threadID=33816&messageID=111558#111557.

5. *Book of Insults, Ancient & Modern*, 18.

6. *Book of Insults, Ancient & Modern*, 20.

7. *The California Tech* website. http://tech.caltech.edu/archive/mit.pdf.

8. Williams and Zadro, 23.

9. Williams and Zadro, 40–43.

10. *Book of Classic Insults*, 4.

11. *Book of Classic Insults*, 5.

12. Adams, 4.

13. Hitchens, 174.

14. Lynch, 7.

15. *Book of Classic Insults*, 128.

16. *Book of Classic Insults*, 120.

17. *Book of Classic Insults*, 112.

18. *Book of Insults, Ancient & Modern*, 99.

19. *Book of Classic Insults*, 114.

20. *Book of Classic Insults*, 44.

21. *Book of Classic Insults*, 44.

22. *Book of Classic Insults*, 62.

23. *Book of Classic Insults*, 89.

24. *Book of Classic Insults*, 50.

25. *Book of Classic Insults*, 49.

26. *Book of Classic Insults*, 50.

27. Grothe, 138.

28. Seneca, "On Anger," III.37.

29. *Book of Classic Insults*, 102.

30. *Book of Classic Insults*, 137.

31. *Book of Classic Insults*, 137.

32. Moore, E1.

Three

1. Grothe, 140.

2. Grothe, 148.

3. Grothe, 29.

4. Bowers, 51.

5. Grothe, 168.

6. *Book of Classic Insults*, 25.
7. Neu, 11. See also the discussion in note 2.

Four

1. Gessen, 194.
2. Gessen, 194.
3. Gessen, 199.
4. Clinton, 341.
5. Grothe, 92.
6. *Book of Classic Insults*, 40.
7. *Book of Classic Insults*, 84.
8. Grothe, 92.
9. *Book of Insults, Ancient & Modern*, 70.
10. Maag, 23.
11. "Justice Sought in Suicide," A34.
12. Zetter, "Lori Drew Not Guilty."
13. Zetter, "Judge Acquits Lori Drew."
14. Plutarch, "How to Tell a Flatterer," 49A.
15. Plutarch, "How to Tell a Flatterer," 56D–E.
16. *Book of Insults, Ancient & Modern*, 67.

Five

1. Kowalski, Howerton, and McKenzie, 186.
2. Kowalski, Howerton, and McKenzie, 191–192.
3. Kowalski, Howerton, and McKenzie, 192.
4. Radcliffe-Brown, 195.
5. Kowalski, Howerton, and McKenzie, 181.
6. Reddy, 254.
7. Kowalski, Howerton, and McKenzie, 186.
8. Kuiper, 206.
9. Kuiper, 206.
10. Kuiper, 207.
11. Keltner, 1231.
12. Kowalski, Howerton, and McKenzie, 177.
13. Keltner, 1232.
14. Kowalski, Howerton, and McKenzie, 189.
15. Abrahams, 209–210.
16. MTV website. "Yo Momma Atlanta: Decatur vs. Westside (Final Round Episode 306)." www.mtv.com/overdrive/?id=1562704&vid=157353.

17. MTV website. "Yo Momma: Ben Hill vs Cabbagetown (Full Episode 303)." http://www.mtv.com/overdrive/?type=1253&id=1560798&vid=151949.
18. Dundes, Leach, and Özkök, 135–136.
19. Dundes, Leach, and Özkök, 137.
20. Dundes, Leach, and Özkök, 136.
21. Dundes, Leach, and Özkök, 157–159.
22. Adams, 105.
23. Adams, 108.
24. Adams, 109.
25. Clinton, 341–343.
26. Garff, 417.
27. Eckert and Newmark, 192.

Six

1. "Beef with Burger King Manager."
2. "Wisconsin Cop."
3. Rasmussen, 21.
4. Leary and Springer, 154.
5. Leary and Springer, 151.
6. Leary and Springer, 165.
7. McDougall et al., 215–216.
8. Rasmussen, 21.
9. Leary et al., "Self-Esteem," 524–525.
10. Leary "Toward a Conceptualization," 7.
11. Leary and Springer, 157.
12. Leary and Springer, 155.
13. Sommer, 167.
14. Brown and Levinson, 321–322.
15. Johnson, S., 535.
16. Williams and Zadro, 26.
17. Kowalski, "Aversive Side," 302.

Seven

1. James, 306.
2. Sommer, 169.
3. Kelly, 303.
4. Sommer, 169.
5. Kelly, 299.

6. Sommer, 169.
7. Sommer, 176.
8. Sommer, 176.
9. Sommer, 168.
10. Campbell, 539.
11. Campbell, 539.
12. Rhodewalt and Morf, 683–684.
13. Baumeister, et al., 84.
14. Marano, 15.
15. "Almost No Blacks," 65.
16. Glod, A01.
17. Twenge, 69.
18. Baumeister et al. develop this argument.

Eight

1. Irvine, *On Desire*.
2. Leary, Koch, and Hechenbleinkner, 147.
3. Leary et al., "Self-Esteem," 519–520.
4. Leary, "Toward a Conceptualization," 10.
5. Leary et al., "Self-Esteem," 528.
6. Leary et al., "Self-Esteem," 528.
7. Leary et al., "Self-Esteem," 520.

Nine

1. Littlewood, 157.
2. Safian, 7.
3. Weintraub, 216.
4. *Book of Classic Insults*, 15.
5. *Book of Classic Insults*, 132.
6. Diogenes Laertius, "Diogenes," VI.49.
7. Grothe, 213.
8. Seneca, "On Anger," III.38.
9. Neu, 58.
10. "Crowe 'Threw More Than Just a Phone,'" 3.
11. McKim, 226.
12. Frevert, 41.
13. Hughes, 41.
14. Hughes, 72.
15. Spierenburg, "Knife Fighting," 114.

16. Frevert, 60.
17. Spierenburg, "Masculinity," 11.
18. Spierenburg, "Masculinity," 10.
19. Seneca, "On Anger," II.32.
20. Seneca, "On Firmness," XIV.3.
21. Seneca, "On Firmness," XVII.3.
22. Epictetus, "Discourses," I.7.30–33.
23. Lynch, 3.
24. Grothe, 238.
25. Seneca, "Happy Life," XXVI.4–5.
26. Seneca, "On Firmness," XII.3.

Ten

1. Elias, 69.
2. Emerson, 7.
3. Greenawalt, 71.
4. Kennedy, 116–117.
5. Hockaway, A1.
6. Greenawalt, 48–49.
7. Greenawalt, 55.
8. *R. A. V. v. City of St. Paul*, 505 U.S. 377 (1992).
9. Greenawalt, 62.
10. *R. v. Keegstra*, 3 S.C.R. 697 (1990).
11. Greenawalt, 68.

Eleven

1. I have defended this assertion in chapter 2 of my *On Desire*.
2. Epictetus, *Handbook*, 13.
3. Musonius Rufus, 10.3
4. Epictetus, *Handbook*, 20.
5. Epictetus, *Handbook*, 30.
6. Marcus Aurelius, XI.13.
7. Diogenes Laertius, "Zeno," VII.6.
8. Musonius Rufus, 9.9; see also the commentary in appendix I of that work.
9. Pliny, 11.
10. See chapter 14 of my *Guide to the Good Life*.
11. Musonius Rufus, 10.3.
12. Epictetus, *Handbook*, 48.
13. Johnson, P., 6.

14. Martin, 483.
15. Epictetus, *Handbook*, 48.
16. Young, 7.
17. Epictetus, *Handbook*, 33.
18. Diogenes Laertius, "Antisthenes," VI.12.
19. Marcus Aurelius, VI.6.
20. Epictetus, *Handbook*, 48.

Twelve

1. Plutarch, "Progress in Virtue," 12.
2. Epictetus, *Handbook*, 48.
3. Seneca, "On the Happy Life," XVII.3.

Works Cited

Abrahams, Roger D. "Playing the Dozens." *Journal of American Folklore* 75, no. 297 (July–September, 1962): 209–220.

Adams, Joey. *Roast of the Town*. New York: Prentice Hall, 1986.

"Almost No Blacks Among the 'Perfect' SAT Scorers." *The Journal of Blacks in Higher Education* 19, (Spring 1998): 65–66.

American Heritage Dictionary of the American Language. Third Edition. Boston: Houghton Mifflin, 1992.

Baumeister, R. F., Jennifer D. Campbell, Joachim I. Krueger, and Kathleen D. Vohs. "Exploding the Self-Esteem Myth." *Scientific American* (January, 2005): 84–91.

"Beef With Burger King Manager Gets Teen Shot." WCBS Television. November 13, 2006. http://wcbstv.com/topstories/burger.king.bronx.2.239799.html.

Bowers, Neal. *Words for the Taking: The Hunt for a Plagiarist*. New York: W. W. Norton, 1997.

Brown, Penelope, and Stephen C. Levinson. "Politeness: Some Universals in Language Usage." In *The Discourse Reader*. Edited by Adam Jaworski and Nikolas Coupland. London: Routledge, 1999.

Campbell, Jennifer D. "Self-Esteem and Clarity of the Self-Concept." *Journal of Personality and Social Psychology* 59, no. 3 (1990): 538–549.

Clinton, Bill. *My Life*. New York: Alfred A. Knopf, 2004.

Cooley, Alison E., and M. G. L. Cooley. *Pompeii: A Sourcebook*. London: Routledge, 2004.

"Crowe 'Threw More Than Just a Phone.'" *The Dominion Post* (Wellington, New Zealand), July 1, 2005, 3.

Diogenes Laertius. "Antisthenes." In *Lives of Eminent Philosophers*. Vol. II. Translated by R. D. Hicks. Cambridge, MA: Harvard University Press, 1925.

——. "Diogenes." In *Lives of Eminent Philosophers*. Vol. II. Translated by R. D. Hicks. Cambridge, MA: Harvard University Press, 1925.

——. "Zeno." In *Lives of Eminent Philosophers*. Vol. II. Translated by R. D. Hicks. Cambridge, MA: Harvard University Press, 1925.

Dundes, Alan, Jerry W. Leach, and Bora Özkök. "The Strategy of Turkish Boys' Verbal Dueling Rhymes." In *Directions in Sociolinguistics: The Ethnography of Communication*. Edited by John J. Gumperz and Dell Hymes. New York: Basil Blackwell, 1986.

Eckert, Penelope, and Russell Newmark. "Central Eskimo Song Duels: A Contextual Analysis of Ritual Ambiguity." *Ethnology* 19, no. 2 (April 1980): 191–211.

Elias, Norbert. *The Civilizing Process: Sociogenetic and Psychogenetic Investigations*. Revised edition. Translated by Edmund Jephcott. Edited by Eric Dunning, Johan Goudsblom, and Stephen Mennell. Malden, MA: Blackwell, 2000.

Emerson, Ralph Waldo. "Manners." In *Essays on Manners, Self-Reliance, Compensation, Nature, Friendship*. Edited by Eunice J. Cleveland. Chicago: Longmans, Green, 1915.

Epictetus. "Discourses." In *Epictetus: The Discourses as Reported by Arrian, the Manual, and Fragments*. 2 vols. Translated by W. A. Oldfather. Cambridge, MA: Harvard University Press, 1925.

——. *Handbook of Epictetus*. Translated by Nicholas White. Indianapolis: Hackett, 1983.

Frevert, Ute. "The Taming of the Noble Ruffian: Male Violence and Dueling in Early Modern and Modern Germany." In *Men and Violence: Gender, Honor, and Rituals in Modern Europe and America*. Edited by Pieter Spierenburg. Columbus: Ohio State University Press, 1998.

Garff, Joakim. *Søren Kierkegaard: A Biography*. Translated by Bruce H. Kirmmse. Princeton, NJ: Princeton University Press, 2005.

Gessen, Masha. *Perfect Rigor: A Genius and the Mathematical Breakthrough of the Century*. Boston: Houghton Mifflin Harcourt, 2009.

Glod, Maria. "High Schools Make Room at Top for Grads; Some Tap Multiple Valedictorians to Cut Rivalry, Spread Honors." *Washington Post*, June 17, 2006: A01.

Greenawalt, Kent. *Fighting Words: Individuals, Communities, and Liberties of Speech*. Princeton, NJ: Princeton University Press, 1995.

Grothe, Mardy. *Vive la Repartee*. New York: HarperCollins, 2005.

Hitchens, Christopher. *Hitch-22: A Memoir*. New York: Hachette, 2010.

Hockaway, James. "In Thailand, Insulting the King Can Mean 15 Years in Jail." *Wall Street Journal*, October 16, 2008. www.online.wsj.com/article/SB122411457349338545.html.

Hughes, Steven. "Men of Steel: Dueling, Honor, and Politics in Liberal Italy." In *Men and Violence: Gender, Honor, and Rituals in Modern Europe and America*. Edited by Pieter Spierenburg. Columbus: Ohio State University Press, 1998.

Irvine, William B. *A Guide to the Good Life: The Ancient Art of Stoic Joy*. New York: Oxford University Press, 2009.

———. *On Desire: Why We Want What We Want*. New York: Oxford University Press, 2006.

James, William. *The Principles of Psychology*. 2007 [1890]. Vol. 1. New York: Cosimo Classics.

Johnson, Paul. *Creators: From Chaucer and Dürer to Picasso and Disney*. New York: HarperCollins, 2006.

Johnson, Samuel. *Johnson and Walker's Critical Pronouncing Dictionary*. New York: Leavitt and Allen, 1862.

"Justice Sought in Suicide After MySpace Hoax." *Newsday,* November 18, 2007. www.newsday.com/news/justice-sought-in-suicide-after-myspace-hoax-1.575884.

Kelly, Kristine M. "Individual Differences in Reactions to Rejection." In *Interpersonal Rejection*. Edited by Mark R. Leary. New York: Oxford University Press, 2001.

Keltner, Dracher, et al. "Teasing in Hierarchical and Intimate Relations." *Journal of Personality and Social Psychology* 75, no. 5 (1988): 1231–1247.

Kennedy, Randall. *Nigger: The Strange Career of a Troublesome Word*. New York: First Vintage, 2003.

Kowalski, Robin M. "Aversive Interpersonal Behaviors: On Being Annoying, Thoughtless, and Mean." In *Behaving Badly: Aversive Behaviors in Interpersonal Relationships*. Edited by Robin M. Kowalski. Washington, DC: American Psychological Association, 2001.

———. "The Aversive Side of Social Interaction Revisited." In *Behaving Badly: Aversive Behaviors in Interpersonal Relationships*. Edited by Robin M. Kowalski. Washington, DC: American Psychological Association, 2001.

Kowalski, Robin M., Elsie Howerton, and Michelle McKenzie. "Permitted Disrespect: Teasing in Interpersonal Interactions." In *Behaving Badly: Aversive Behaviors in Interpersonal Relationships*. Edited by Robin M. Kowalski. Washington, DC: American Psychological Association, 2001.

Kuiper, Koenraad. "Sporting Formulae in New Zealand English: Two Models of Male Solidarity." In *English Around the World: Sociolinguistic Perspectives*. Edited by Jenny Cheshire. Cambridge: Cambridge University Press, 1991.

Leary, Mark R. "Toward a Conceptualization of Interpersonal Rejection." In *Interpersonal Rejection*. Edited by Mark R. Leary. New York: Oxford University Press, 2001.

Leary, Mark R., Erika J. Koch, and Nancy R. Hechenbleikner. "Emotional Responses to Interpersonal Rejection." In *Interpersonal Rejection*. Edited by Mark R. Leary. New York: Oxford University Press, 2001.

Leary, Mark R., and Carrie A. Springer. "Hurt Feelings: The Neglected Emotion." In *Behaving Badly: Aversive Behaviors in Interpersonal Relationships*. Edited by Robin M. Kowalski. Washington, DC: American Psychological Association, 2001.

Leary, Mark R., Ellen S. Tambor, Sonja K. Terdal, and Deborah L. Downs. "Self-Esteem as an Interpersonal Monitor: The Sociometer Hypothesis." *Journal of Personality and Social Psychology* 68, no. 3 (March, 1995): 518–530.

Littlewood, John Edensor. *Littlewood's Miscellany*. Edited by Béla Bollobás. New York: Cambridge University Press, 1986.

Lynch, Jack. Introduction to *Samuel Johnson's Insults*. New York: Walker, 2004.

Maag, Christopher. "A Hoax Turned Fatal Draws Anger but No Charges." *The New York Times*, November 28, 2007. www.nytimes.com/2007/11/28/us/28hoax.html.

Marano, Hara Estroff. *A Nation of Wimps: The High Cost of Invasive Parenting*. New York: Broadway Books, 2008.

Marcus Aurelius. *Meditations*. Translated by Maxwell Staniforth. London: Penguin, 1964.

Martin, Stanley. *The Order of Merit: One Hundred Years of Matchless Honour*. London: I. B. Tauris, 2007.

McDougall, Patricia, Shelley Hymel, Tracy Vaillancourt, and Louise Mercer. "The Consequences of Childhood Peer Rejection." In *Interpersonal Rejection*. Edited by Mark R. Leary. New York: Oxford University Press, 2001.

McKim, W. Duncan. *A Study for the Times: An Inquiry into Thought and Motive*. New York: G. P. Putnam's Sons, 1920.

McPhee, Nancy. *The Book of Insults, Ancient & Modern*. New York: St. Martin's Press, 1978.

Mencken, H. L. *Prejudices: Fourth Series*. New York: Knopf, 1924.

Moore, Molly. "Zidane Says 'Harsh' Insults By Italian Led to Head Butt." *The Washington Post*, July 13, 2006. http://www.washingtonpost.com/wp-dyn/content/article/2006/07/12/AR2006071201184.html.

Musonius Rufus. *Musonius Rufus: The Lectures and Sayings*. Translated by Cynthia King. N.p.: Lulu, 2010.

Neu, Jerome. *Sticks and Stones: The Philosophy of Insults*. New York: Oxford University Press, 2008.

New English Bible with the Apocrypha. Oxford: Oxford University Press, 1970.

Pliny. *Letters of Pliny*. Translated by William Melmoth. Revised by F. C. T. Bosanquet. Middlesex, UK: The Echo Library, 2006.

Plutarch. "How a Man May Become Aware of His Progress in Virtue." In *Plutarch's Moralia*. Vol. 1. Translated by Frank Cole Babbitt. Cambridge, MA: Harvard University Press, 1927.

———. "How to Tell a Flatterer from a Friend." In *Plutarch's Moralia*. Vol. 1. Translated by Frank Cole Babbitt. Cambridge, MA: Harvard University Press, 1927.

Price, Steven D. Introduction to *1001 Insults, Put-Downs, and Come-Backs*. Guilford, CT: The Lyons Press, 2005.

Radcliffe-Brown, Alfred. "On Joking Relationships." *Africa: Journal of the International African Institute* 13, no. 3 (July 1940): 195–210.

Rasmussen, Knud. *The Netsilik Eskimos: Social Life and Spiritual Culture*. Copenhagen: Gyldendalske Boghandel, Nordisk Forlag, 1931.

Reddy, Vasudevi. "Infant Clowns: The Interpersonal Creation of Humour in Infancy." *Enfance* 53, no. 3 (2001): 247–256.

Rhodewalt, Frederick, and Carolyn C. Morf. "On Self-Aggrandizement and Anger: A Temporal Analysis of Narcissism and Affective Reactions to Success and Failure." *Journal of Personality and Social Psychology* 74, no. 3 (1998): 672–685.

Safian, Louis A. Introduction to *2,000 Insults for All Occasions*. Secaucus, NJ: Citadel Press, 1965.

Seneca. "On Anger." In *Moral and Political Essays*. Translated by John M. Cooper and J. F. Procopé. Cambridge: Cambridge University Press, 1995.

———. "On Firmness." In *Moral Essays*. Vol. I. Translated by John W. Basore. Cambridge, MA: Harvard University Press, 1928.

———. "On the Happy Life." In *Moral Essays*. Vol. II. Translated by John W. Basore. Cambridge, MA: Harvard University Press, 1932.

Shakespeare, William. *The Tragedy of King Lear*. Edited by George Lyman Kittredge. Waltham, MA: Blaisdell Publishing, 1967.

Sommer, Kristin. "Coping with Rejection: Ego-Defensive Strategies, Self-Esteem, and Interpersonal Relationships." In *Interpersonal Rejection*. Edited by Mark R. Leary. New York: Oxford University Press, 2001.

Spierenburg, Pieter. "Knife Fighting and Popular Codes of Honor in Early Modern Amsterdam." In *Men and Violence: Gender, Honor, and Rituals in Modern Europe and America*. Edited by Pieter Spierenburg. Columbus: Ohio State University Press, 1998.

——. "Masculinity, Violence, and Honor: An Introduction." In *Men and Violence: Gender, Honor, and Rituals in Modern Europe and America*. Edited by Pieter Spierenburg. Columbus: Ohio State University Press, 1998.

Steele, Tom, ed. *The Book of Classic Insults*. New York: William Morrow, 1999.

Tedeschi, James T., and Michael Harris Bond. "Aversive Behavior and Aggression in Cultural Perspective." In *Behaving Badly: Aversive Behaviors in Interpersonal Relationships*. Edited by Robin M. Kowalski. Washington, DC: American Psychological Association, 2001.

Twenge, Jean M. *Generation Me: Why Today's Young Americans Are More Confident, Assertive, Entitled—And More Miserable than Ever Before*. New York: Free Press, 2006.

Weintraub, Stanley. *Shaw's People: Victoria to Churchill*. University Park, PA: Pennsylvania University Press, 1996.

Williams, Kipling D., and Lisa Zadro. "Ostracism: On Being Ignored, Excluded, and Rejected." In *Interpersonal Rejection*. Edited by Mark R. Leary. New York: Oxford University Press, 2001.

"Wisconsin Cop Snapped After Being Called a 'Worthless Pig.'" October 9, 2007. *NY Daily News*. www.nydailynews.com/news/ny_crime/2007/10/09/2007-10-09_wisconsin_cop_snapped_after_being_called-1.html.

Young, Laurence. *Mathematicians and their Times*. Edited by Leopoldo Nachbin. Amsterdam: North-Holland, 1981.

Zetter, Kim. "Judge Acquits Lori Drew in Cyberbullying Case, Overrules Jury." *Wired*, July 2, 2009. www.wired.com/threatlevel/2009/07/drew_court/.

——. "Lori Drew Not Guilty of Felonies in Landmark Cyberbullying Trial." *Wired*, November 16, 2008. www.wired.com/threatlevel/2008/11/lori-drew-pla-5/.

Index